NOT MY Mother's Fault

By
Sally N. Samczyk (Stilson)

PublishAmerica
Baltimore

First printing

At the specific preference of the author, PublishAmerica allowed this work to remain exactly as the author intended, verbatim, without editorial input.

ISBN: 1-4137-8085-7
PUBLISHED BY PUBLISHAMERICA, LLLP
www.publishamerica.com
Baltimore

Printed in the United States of America

I dedicate this book to my mom for never giving up on me when I needed her the most. To my children, who have been patient with me while I was writing this story. To Ron, for loving me and believing in me and giving me the courage to finish this story. And, to the rest of my family. I love you all.

CHAPTER 1

It all started in the fall of 1976. It was almost Halloween when I thought my world had collapsed around me.

It was the day my father walked out and left my mom and his five kids behind. When he went, he left my mom with no money, no food, nothing. Mom had no idea how she was going to raise five kids. I was only seven at the time, but I understood what was going on.

I was angry at Dad for walking out and leaving me behind. I loved my mom, but I loved my dad more. I was really close to him. He was always my idol. Except when he beat on my mother or one of us kids.

My dad was an alcoholic, and he used to come home drunk and beat Mom, and sometimes if he couldn't get all of his anger out on Mom, he would start on us kids. Sometimes I thought I hated him when he was like that. But then he always said he was sorry, and I forgave him.

After Dad left, I cried a lot at first. I missed him a lot. At times I couldn't believe he was gone. I hoped he would come home some day and be a different man.

I wouldn't tell Mom what I was feeling. I was afraid she would tell me to grow up and face it that Dad wasn't coming home again. I couldn't deal with the thought he would never come back.

A couple of months later, Mom had to move to a different place because the one we were living in had been sold. But that still wouldn't make me understand why we had to move. I was afraid that once we moved, Dad would never find where we lived.

Soon after we moved into the new house, Mom got a job. She told us she had to so she could support us. I was scared that once she started working, she might leave just like Dad did, and that scared the hell out of me. I started nagging her, wanting her to stay home, and she got so angry with me that she sent me to my room. I never told Mom how I felt. I kept everything bottled up. I was too scared of being made fun of.

Mom was never a mean person. She was always loving and caring. Instead of hitting us kids, she sent us to our rooms most of the time.

The house we lived in had a creek behind it, and that was where I spent a lot of my time, catching frogs and playing in the water. But then a lot of times, I sat on this huge log that was across the creek and thought of the day that Dad would come home. But he never did.

Slowly the years started passing by, but I never gave up hope that he would come home. I did stop crying. But I was still feeling hurt and alone, and I started wanting to be alone all the time. I never wanted anyone around me. As long as everyone let me be, no one had trouble with me, but once they tried to corner me, I went ape. No one could really control me once I got out of hand. Mom tried, but I didn't let her reach me. She started giving up and just walking away.

After several years had passed, Mom met a guy, Larry. I hated him right away. I didn't give him a chance to get to know me. Each time he tried to talk to me, I told him to get away and not to bother me. But things really started getting hairy when he started coming around all the time. I hated it. I thought he was trying to take my dad's place, and I wasn't going to give him a chance. I always made that poor man's life hell whenever he came around me.

But one day, Mom and Larry came into the living room and said they had something to tell us kids. My oldest brother turned off the TV, and we all turned to look at them. Mom, as always when she was with him, was smiling. But there was something she was going to say, and I knew I was not going to like it.

"Kids, Larry and I have decided that we're going to live together. You five kids and I will move into his big farmhouse."

She looked at me when I got up off the floor. I made a mistake that day when I opened my mouth.

"You can't move in with him. You don't even know if Dad is going to come home or not." I went to run past her, but she caught me by the arm.

"Sally, your dad is never coming home. You have got to accept that. It's been five years since he walked out, and he's never coming back."

I put my hands over my ears so I didn't have to hear any more and ran out the door and down to the creek.

I sat on the edge of the creek, and at first I sat there crying. Then I screamed, and when my throat hurt from doing both, I curled up into a ball and lay there on the ground.

I made a vow that day that I would never cry again over my dad. To me that day, and any other day, he was considered dead. But that didn't help matters when I went to the house that night. Larry had gone, never to come back. I should have been glad, but I didn't feel anything. Only anger at myself for hurting my mom the way I did.

One year later, Mom bought a new house in town. It was closer to where she worked. I was excited, but scared because not only was I leaving my friends from school behind, but I would have no place to go and think any longer. I was going to miss the creek and the country.

CHAPTER 2

At first, I hated living in town. It was too noisy for me. I could remember only one other time that we lived in town, and I hated it then, too. I preferred the peace and quiet of the country. But after a while I got used to the new town and found that it had an arcade. And that's where I met my new friends.

Meeting them was a huge mistake. Everyone was so much older then I, but they took me in as if my age didn't matter. And that's where I met Sandy. She was real cool. She was only sixteen, and she was fun to be around. I started hanging with her and her friends. I started drinking and smoking joints with them and staying out until late at night. Sandy and the other girls knew some people who would buy for them, so it wasn't hard to get what we wanted.

Mom and I started arguing and fighting all the time. I no longer cared if I hurt her or not. I thought I had found people who really understood me, even though they really didn't know anything about me. Mom thought I was too young to be staying out so late, and that caused one of our biggest fights. I started not coming home until she was either at work or asleep. And each time I came down off the high of the drugs or from drinking, I always felt sorry for hurting Mom. I thought I didn't care, but I did.

Then one day while I was at the arcade with my friends, I noticed this guy who came walking into the place. I happened to be over at the jukebox playing some songs, and when he came in I looked up and thought I was looking at the cutest guy I had ever laid eyes on. He had a crewcut and his hair was brown. He had blue eyes and was about five-ten and about a hundred and sixty pounds. He didn't notice me standing there looking at him like I had never seen a guy before. I wanted to meet him, so I went over to where Sandy was sitting at the table.

"Sandy, come here for a minute." She got up and walked over to the jukebox with me.

Pointing my finger over toward the guy, I asked her, "Who's that guy right there with the black T-shirt and black jeans on?" She looked at me not really sure what to say.

"Sally, don't bother with him 'cause be won't have nothing to do with you because of your age." I looked at her like she was crazy.

"What the hell do you mean? No one knows my age. You know that." I gave her a dirty look.

"You really don't know who that is, do you?" she said.

I shook my head. I had never laid eyes on him before, so how was I supposed to know him?

"He's been to your house before, Sally. He's your sister's boyfriend's best friend."

I wouldn't have known that. I was never at home to find out who was going out with who. I never took that much interest before. I thought about it for a couple of seconds, but I could never place him at my house.

"Take me over to him, anyway. He can't hurt me, so what's the big deal?"

She rolled her eyes and finally gave in. "Come on, you little pipsqueak." I had to laugh 'cause she had called me that since I met her. I had always been short, so it really never bothered me.

"Watch it, Sandy."

She laughed, and I followed her over to where he was playing pinball. I was a little surprised because he was playing the same game that I always played when I did play. We waited until he was done with the game, and then Sandy started talking to him.

"Hey, Tom. What's up?"

They talked for a couple of minutes before she introduced me to him.

"Tom, this my good friend Sally."

He smiled, but he really didn't say anything. I was hurt and couldn't figure that out. I didn't know the guy, but I still was hurt, and that made me angry.

"I've really got to go, Sandy. I'll catch you later."

She smiled 'cause I think she knew I was upset. I walked out of the arcade and went into the alley. I figured I would walk for a while, then maybe if I felt up to it, I would go home early and surprise my mom for once. But halfway through the alley, I came upon a guy who hung out with the crowd that I hung with.

"Hey, Sally. What are you doing out here? You ain't going home, are you?"

I smiled at him.

"Yeah, I was thinking about it. Why? What are you guys doing out here?"

He smiled and brought out a joint. I should have known.

"Well, you guys have fun, and I will just pretend like I never saw a thing." I started walking away when Todd stopped me.

"What's your rush? Come on over here and smoke it with me."

He put his arm around my shoulder and walked me back to the car they were sitting on.

Todd and I got together after that. I started spending all of my time with him. At first, things seemed to be going pretty well between us, up until he started telling me what I could do and what I could wear. That pissed me off. No one was going to tell me what I could do and what I had to wear. So I defied him. He started to push me around, but it was nothing real serious, or at least I didn't think so. But one night, he took it too far. I had gone over to his house 'cause we were going to go to a party together. I was all decked out. I thought I looked really nice, but Todd did not want me to be looking like I did.

"Are you ready to go, Todd?"

When he turned around and looked at me, his face went pure red.

"You're not going to no party looking like that. What do you want to do, find someone else?"

That thought had never crossed my mind.

"What's your problem? I've always dressed like this. It's not like my jeans are too tight or my shirt is too low."

He was being just too obnoxious.

"Yeah, and how many times have I told you not to dress that way?"

Boy, he was really pissing me off.

"Yeah, well you aren't my father, either."

I should have never said that 'cause the next thing I knew, he was hitting me and pushing me around. I think I was called every name in the book that day. He knocked me around pretty good that day. But I wasn't one to stick around and take another beating. At the first chance I got, I took off out the door and down the road. I couldn't go home. Mom would really freak out. I had blood coming from my nose, and my lip was busted open. Plus, there were all the bruises that would show up by the next day. I could already feel my eye starting to swell shut.

The first place I went to was the park, and I sat on the table thinking of the last time I could ever remember taking a beating like that. It was just before my dad left. My younger sister had done something wrong, and Dad was hitting her pretty good. I could still hear her screams at each hit she took. I ran up to Dad and started screaming at him to leave her alone. I got the worst beating of my life that day. But I couldn't have handled it if anything would have happened to my sister.

I still had no idea of where I was going to go. I thought about going to Sandy's, but I hadn't really hung with her since I started going out with Todd. She had upset me when she told me Todd was bad news. Todd and I used to do all sorts of different drugs. My favorite was cocaine. I didn't shoot up like he did. Instead, I snorted it. I didn't do it that often to be hooked, but I could have done it every day if I could have afforded it. But Todd always had it, so I never had to worry about where I was going to get it. Whatever drugs Todd had, that's what I did. Sandy knew I was getting in way too deep, but she never said anything to me except that I should be more careful.

Finally, I decided I would go to her. The worst thing she could do was tell me to go home. I wouldn't have blamed her if she would have. I walked to her house and knocked on her door. I thought for sure her mother was going to answer. But it was Sandy who opened the door. As soon as she let me in the door, she noticed what I looked like.

"Sally, what the hell happened to you?"

She still cared, even though I treated her like crap. I knew then she was a true friend.

"Nothing. I just got into a little fight. That's all."

I tried to smile, but it hurt too much.

"A little fight? Well, it looks like they got the best of you this time."

I wouldn't tell her it was Todd.

"Yeah. Well, I'll be OK. I just need a little help on getting cleaned up. Do you mind?"

I was waiting for her to try and get it out of me who it was I had got into the fight with. Instead, she motioned for me to follow her into the bathroom.

She helped me get all the dried blood off my face and gave me some ice to put on my eye. I thought I was in the clear about her asking me who it was. But after we had got all over with the cleaning up, she took me to the bedroom and had me sit down on the bed.

"Sally, this isn't one of your normal fights you usually get into. So why don't you tell me who it was? I think I already know, but I want you to tell me."

I sat there for a couple of minutes trying to figure out who I could tell her it was. But before I could say anything, she spoke up.

"It was Todd. Wasn't it?" She sat there waiting for me to confirm what she already knew.

"Sandy, just leave it alone. Ok? I'm all right, and I just want to put it all behind me."

"No one that beats up a girl should just get away with it."

I agreed with her, but I was afraid he would come back for me.

"Sandy, if you really are my friend, then you'll just leave it alone."

She stood up and looked me right in the face.

"Sally, I am your friend. I may not have agreed with everything you do, but I am your friend, and that's why that little creep won't get away with what he's done."

I could do nothing to change her mind. So finally I just gave up.

Mom never said anything about my black and blue eye, and I never offered to tell her. But the next time I saw Todd, he wasn't looking too pretty. He even tried to get me to go back to him, telling me he would never do it again and going on and on about how sorry he was. But I wouldn't budge. I was never going to go through something like that again.

CHAPTER 3

A couple of months later, things were getting worse. School started, and I didn't want to go back. Mom and I hardly ever spoke, and I was spending most of my time at Sandy's. But to me, she was starting to get too close to me, and that bothered me a lot. I hated for people to get too close. I liked them as long as they didn't really know me.

I started hanging out at the arcade, going out with guys I had never met before, and staying out all night, sometimes being dropped off at the door not sure of how I even got there. But one night, Mom couldn't stand it anymore. When I was brought home, I was flung onto the porch and left there until I could get up and go into the house. Mom had to come out and help me in.

By the time Mom got done with me that night, I knew from all the hitting that I would feel it come morning. She finally left me on the floor to sleep it off. She kept screaming at me that I was becoming nothing but a dope addict and a drunk. I passed out.

The next morning, Mom got me up early and wanted me to sit at the table so she could talk to me. I got up and went out, still half asleep. But she caught my attention when she started talking, and I could hear the pain in her voice.

"Sally, I don't understand why you think you have to be this way and why you hate me so much."

I looked at her.

"I don't hate you, Mom."

"Well, you sure as hell act like you do. Sally, you are my daughter, and I love you just like I love the others, and that's why I think you need to get some help. I'm not saying it to make you upset. I'm telling you this 'cause I love you, and I hate to see you throwing your life away like you are."

I sat there listening to her. But the more she said, the more upset I got. I could feel my face growing real red.

"Mom, I didn't ask you to sit here with me. I did not ask you to sit here and have this little talk with me. So how can you sit there and tell me I'm throwing my life away."

I got up to walk away from the table. This time, not once while I was talking to her did I raise my voice to her. But before I left the room, I had to tell her one more thing.

"You know, Mom, I may be your daughter, but I wish I would have never been born. I hate this life. It's full of nothing but heartache. But if I could go back and be reborn, I would not have picked a different mother." With that I walked away.

I walked around for a long time that day just walking and thinking about what Mom had said about getting some help. I knew she was right. I did need some help, but I was not the type of person to go and ask people for help. For the first time, I was going to ask Mom for help, and maybe I could get my crap together.

When I went back to the house, I couldn't believe what I saw. I walked into the living room, and Tom was sitting on the couch watching TV. I stared at him for a few minutes, then I looked over at my sister and her boyfriend, and still I could not believe Sandy was right.

"Hey, do you know where Ma went to?" I asked my sister.

She didn't know either, so I went to my room and sat on the bed. Seeing Tom there blew my mind, and I was almost to the point that I was going to say the hell with it and just go get plastered, but I really was in no mood to go out. I wanted to stay home, but I felt out of place. So I went over to Sandy's and sat there drinking a little. I had already lost my nerve that night to ask Mom for help, so I didn't go home at all.

I stayed away from the house for a couple of days. I let Mom know where I was 'cause I didn't want her to think I had gone and gotten myself killed or something. But I had to get my head together and make sure I would get some help. I needed to talk to someone I could trust, but I knew of no one I trusted with my deepest feelings. When I went back to Mom's, I walked into the house and was going to ask Mom to help me to get the help I needed but again Tom and everyone else was there. When I walked in and stood by the doorway, everyone looked at me like some sort of oddball. They weren't used to seeing me home at night or, hell, not that often during the daytime, either.

"Don't you guys have something better to stare at?" I said, joking around with them. But my sister had to come back with something.

"Not really. We don't know if we even know who you are." She was trying to be funny, but I didn't find that too funny. I never got along with her. She did her thing, and I did mine. The only ones I really had anything to do with were my younger brother and sister. I felt close to them to a point, but I would never even let them too close.

Mom got off the couch and came walking up to me with a smile on her face. I knew she was happy I had decided I would be home for a change, even though she still was unsure.

"So, are you home for the night or are you leaving again?"

I could tell that she really wanted me there.

"I'm home for the night. But after the house clears out, I want to talk to you alone."

She was puzzled. I could tell by her face. But she didn't say anything.

By the time everyone cleared out, I was pretty tired, but I stayed up with Mom, talking to her. I told her I thought if I could get some counseling, then I thought I could get my head together. She agreed with me. I felt so good about talking to Mom, I thought we finally had made amends.

CHAPTER 4

I got the counseling I needed and was doing real well. For eight months straight, I had my act together. I still argued with Mom but not like I used to. I could even go to parties and not drink or do anything. I was really proud of myself. But then everything started to fall apart. I had gone to my session like I always did. I never missed one. And this was one I wished I would have missed.

Walking into the office, I walked into a big mess. There was boxes and papers and all sorts of stuff all around. The office was always nice and tidy, so when I walked in, I knew there was something wrong. I looked over at Mr. Fox.

"Boy, this is a change. What's up?"

"Sit down, Sally." He cleared off the chair I always sat on.

"What's going on, Mr. Fox? I've never seen your office looking like this."

I tried to laugh, but I was afraid of what he was going to tell me.

"Sally, this will be our last session together. I'm moving and someone else is going to take over my job here."

He was being transferred to someplace else. I thought I had just lost my best friend. I went running out of the office, and I never went back.

As long as I was in my sessions, I was home all the time. I even got to know Tom a little. He was bright and funny, and I could tell he was a very loving and caring person. I fell head over heels in love with him. I think I would have done anything for him. He didn't look at me like I looked at him, so I couldn't just come out and tell him what I felt, but I'm almost positive he knew how I felt. He was the first guy I truly can say captured my heart and made me think twice about what I was going to do now that my counselor was gone.

I started drinking again and wanting to stay out until all hours of the night. I left the drugs alone, except every once in a while I smoked a joint. But I wasn't going to let myself get like I was. Hell, even I hated doing what I was doing.

When I was at the arcade one night, it was pretty well deserted, so I had the whole place to myself with no others to bother me. I talked to the lady who worked behind the counter and then went over to the jukebox so I could listen to some music. "Crimson and Clover" had just begun, and I was selecting some other songs to play when I got a tap on the shoulder. When I turned around, it was Tom.

"Hey, girl, what are you doing up here all by yourself? I thought you would have gone to that big party your friends went to?"

"Nah, not tonight. I didn't feel up to it. I thought I would play a little pinball, then go on home."

"That's a change. You haven't been around home that much in a month."

I just looked at him. It felt good to know he knew how long it was since I quit being around home. We talked for a while, and I knew I would never be good enough for him, being the way I was. I wanted him to love me, but I knew he never would as long as I was the way I was.

I went home after that and talked to Mom about going somewhere to live. Anywhere but around that town. She had no idea where I would go at first, then it hit her that my aunt would most likely let me go there.

It was hard to leave that town. I wanted to cry, but I thought I was doing the right thing. So I lifted my chin and silently I told Tom goodbye. He was the main one I was going to miss.

Staying at my aunt's house was a mistake, however. Her three kids were good, and I grew to love them dearly, but I needed some time to myself, and with her always gone, there was no way I could. I bathed the kids and fed them their supper and put them to bed. Then I would do my homework and get ready for bed myself. It all grew to be real old.

In November of that year, I met this guy. He would never be like Tom, but he was sweet.

Sue was one of the girls I met at school and became close friends with. She and I were supposed to go the school dance together. She was coming over to my house to spend the night, and we were to go to the dance from there. My aunt and uncle were taking us, and when the dance was over, they were going to pick us up.

They dropped us off in front of the school, and when they saw we were going into the building, they pulled away. As soon as they were out of sight, we took off to go uptown. I was surprised this place even had an arcade. And that's where I was heading.

We laughed and joked and were just having a lot of fun. I would never have imagined you could have fun without booze or something to lift you up. But we were having a good time. And when I saw a guy across the room, I had even more fun. He wasn't my usual type, but, hell, I wanted someone, and he was cute enough.

I sat on the picnic table watching him play pool. He was skinny and not very tall, but he had a cuteness about him that attracted me to him. He came over to where Sue and I were sitting and sat down between us. Sue already knew him, and I wanted her to introduce me to him.

"Hey, Pete. I want you to meet a good friend of mine, Sally."

"Hi. I've never seen you around here before. Where you from?"

He was a nice guy, blond, blue eyes, and all. He couldn't measure up to Tom, but I thought given time, I would like this guy a lot.

That's when Pete and I got together. He either called me every night, or I called him. We talked about everything, no matter how small. He was very giving and loving, and very caring. He listened to my complaints about my aunt always leaving the kids for me to take care of. He was the only person besides my counselor who really listened to what I had to say.

When Thanksgiving came around, Pete wanted me to go to his house, but of course I couldn't because Mom was having the family dinner. I would like to have gone to Pete's house to meet his parents, out of curiosity, but I thought I would have more time later to meet them.

Going to Mom's for dinner was not something I really wanted to do. I could never get along with her side of the family. But I was looking forward to seeing Mom and my brothers and sisters.

I was even happier than I thought I would be about seeing Mom. When I first walked in, I gave her a big hug and a kiss on the cheek. She looked at me in total surprise.

"What was that for? You haven't done that since you were . . . . Damn. I can't remember when." She laughed and hugged me back. I walked away from her laughing.

I stuck around the house for a couple of hours, but being around everyone was starting to give me a huge headache. I figured it was time to get out of there for a while. I went to find Mom.

"Mom, would you mind if I took off for a little bit? I'm getting a slight headache from being around everyone." She stood there by the sink looking at me with a dish in her hand. I could tell she really didn't want me to go anywhere.

"Come on, Mom. I won't get into trouble. I just want to get out of this madhouse. I promise." She hesitated.

"All right. You can go, but I don't want you to go hanging with them people you were hanging with. That's what gets you into trouble. All right?"

I agreed. I grabbed my coat and went out the door.

I went to the arcade like I always did, but no one was there except the woman who worked behind the counter.

"Pretty dead tonight, huh?" I asked her.

"Yeah. But where have you been? I haven't seen you come in here for a while." She was always a nice lady.

"Well, I don't live around here no more." I wouldn't tell her any more. I didn't think it was any of her business. I got my tokens and walked away. I went first to the jukebox and put on some music, then I went over to the pinball games. I must have been there for only about a half-hour when I got a tap on the shoulder. I turned around to see who it was.

"Hey, guy. What's up?" I was so surprised 'cause he was the last guy I thought I would see in there that day.

"Not a whole lot. I thought I would stop in and play a few games before heading home," Tom said with that sexy voice that always made me go weak in the knees.

"Well, I'm almost done. Then you can have the whole game to yourself." Now that he was there, I thought I would head on back sooner than I had planned.

"Why don't you stick around so that we can talk and play a few games together."

I looked at him. He had never given me a reason to believe he wanted me around.

I stayed there for a while enjoying being around him. We laughed and joked about the game we were playing, just having fun. I was head over heels for this guy, but I knew he would never feel the same for me. And that made me start thinking about Pete. What would he say if he knew I was in the arcade with someone I wanted to go out with?

"Well, Tom, it was great seeing you again. But I really have to be going home. I told Mom I wouldn't be gone long." I smiled as I put my coat on and started heading out the door. I had to get away from him. He scared me in a way. Not that he would hurt me on purpose. But I still carried a torch for him. I most likely always would.

"Sally. Wait. Let me give you a lift home. It's cold out there." I wanted to cry 'cause I knew it would be my last time to see him and be close to him.

"All right, Tom."

He never drove anything fancy, and I liked him for being just himself. I was glad I wasn't one of those girls who thought you had to have fancy things or they wouldn't have anything to do with you.

He had to take a lap through town. It was like the arcade, deserted. I sat there smelling his cologne and being in his car. I wanted more than anything to get out right then and there and go home. Finally, when he did take me home, I wanted to get out of his car and leave him behind and try to get over him. But he didn't want me to get out of his car just yet.

"You know, Sally, it's not the same around this town since you left." He looked over at me and smiled.

"Well, I'm not going to come back. I can't."

"Why not? You know, you're different from all the girls around here. You may act like a coldhearted bitch, but I think you're a very loving person, if you just let yourself be." That's when he really scared me. I didn't want anyone to know me that well.

"For one thing, I never want to come back here. And second, I can be the coldest bitch you will ever know." My temper was rising.

"Sally, why do you want to keep everyone away? I've watched you for a long time, and each time someone starts getting close to you or even wants to get close, you pull away and want to run. You know, not everyone out there is out to hurt you." For someone who never talked that much, he sure was letting his mouth run.

"Hey, Tom, look, you can think whatever you want. I don't really care. But we had a nice day, and I can't figure out why you want to ruin it by talking about stuff that doesn't concern you. So, come on, leave it all alone." He looked at me and I thought for sure he was still going to pick at me, but he didn't.

"All right. You win this time, but you won't the next. And you will see one day I'm right."

"Well, we will see," I told him. He laughed. After we got off that subject, we had a pretty good time. We had been sitting there in his car in the driveway talking for some time, and when we looked over at the house, we realized we hadn't noticed that everyone in the house was watching us. We started laughing.

"Well, Tom, it was fun, but I think I better be getting in the house." I opened the door and stood there for a second.

"Goodbye, Tom. You take care of yourself."

Before he could say anything, I closed the door and ran into the house. I hadn't realized I had been gone that long, but it had been longer than I thought 'cause dinner was already over, and they were cleaning up. I wasn't hungry, so I didn't bother to get anything to eat. I was in a depressing mood.

CHAPTER 5

Mom had wanted me to stick around until Thanksgiving vacation was over, but I didn't want to be around in case Tom came back. So I went back to my aunt's house.

Once I was back at my aunt's house, I wished I would have taken the chance of running into Tom. At least I would have had some freedom. The only thing that made it bearable was Pete.

I never would forget about Tom, and I would never give that part of my heart to someone else, but I had to put him in the back of my mind.

I never told Pete about Tom. As far as he was concerned, there was no Tom. I gave Pete a chance like I never gave anyone. I gave him my trust, and he gave me his. He never put me down about anything, and finally when I thought I could tell him, I told him about my father. He didn't say much, but he did say he would like to come face to face with my father one time so he could tell him what kind of louse he was.

I thought everything was going well between Pete and me, even though things were pretty bad between me and my aunt and my uncle. I was always fighting with them about leaving me alone with the kids all the time. I didn't think it was right that she was always spending most of her time at the bar. I was getting the feeling she only wanted me there so she didn't have to get a babysitter.

When I came home from school one afternoon, the phone was ringing. I thought it was Pete 'cause he always called me as soon as he knew I was home. After I spoke into the phone, the voice that came back at me was not Pete's.

"Hello, Sally. Do you know who this is?" Whoever it was, he had a deep voice.

"No, I don't know who you are, and I don't know what you want. So, why don't you just tell me?"

"Sally, I'm your father. How are you doing?"

I was in total shock. After all these years, he finally called. The first thing that popped into my head was, what did he want?

"Sally, are you there?"

"Yeah, I'm here. How are you doing? It's been a long time since I've heard from you?"

"Yeah, well, now I'm calling." He asked how I was and told me Mom told him everything I had done. I was very angry at Mom 'cause I didn't think she had any business telling him anything about me.

"Yeah, well, Dad, you know the saying, 'Shit happens.' I got in with the wrong friends, and now I'm paying the price. So if you want to start on someone, don't try doing it to me; find someone else. I live with it every day. I live with it being thrown into my face that I was a drug addict and a drunk. So if you called me to give me more shit, then you wasted your time."

I hadn't meant to be so rude, but if he wanted to start in on me, then I was going to come right out and tell him what I thought. I felt he had no right telling me about anything. It was his fault that he walked out and left me.

"I didn't call you to start a fight, Sally. I called you to see how you're doing."

Once he understood where I stood, we had a nice talk. We talked about everything. I hadn't realized I still missed him. Just before we were about to hang up, he asked me something I couldn't believe he asked.

"Sally, would you like to come out here and live with me? You would like Arizona. It's a lot warmer than Michigan."

I didn't know what to say at first. I like the idea of leaving Michigan, but I didn't know about going down there with him. It had been a long time since I last saw him. The main thing I was concerned about was his drinking.

"Do you still drink, Dad? I mean, like you used to?" I had to know because if he did, then there was no way I was going to go.

"No, Sally. I only drink on occasion. I haven't drank like that in years."

I believed him. He made it sound so convincing.

"I'm glad to hear that. But could I have some time to think about it?"

I wanted to go so I could get to know my dad once more, but I still feared him.

"You sure can. I'll call you next Saturday, and you can tell me then. All right?"

I agreed and we hung up. I had a lot to think about, and I couldn't do it sitting there on the couch. Whenever I had a lot on my mind, I liked to walk and be alone. The only problem was there was no one to watch the kids, and I wouldn't leave them alone. So I decided I would take the three kids and let them play outside.

The phone was ringing when we came in out of the cold. I was out there for less than an hour 'cause the kids were getting cold, and I didn't want them to get sick on me. When I picked up the phone and heard Pete's voice on the other end, it dawned on me that I wasn't in when he tried to call me earlier. And then, with me being on the phone with Dad, he most likely was worrying about where I was.

"What the hell is going on? I've been trying to get a hold of you for over an hour. First I got a busy signal, then I didn't get no answer at all."

I wasn't ready to tell him about Dad yet.

"I took the kids out to play. I got them to have a snowball fight. We were having fun."

I got him talking about being outside, so he forgot about the phone being busy.

I made my decision the day before Dad was to call. I had come home from school like I always did, and I wasn't in the door five minutes when the phone started ringing. It was my aunt.

"Sally, I'm not going to be home until late. I'm going out with some friends of mine."

That pissed me off.

"Who the hell do you think you are? You're always going out, leaving me with the kids. Don't you think you should stay home once in a while to take care of them?" I was very angry with her.

"I will do whatever I want to do. I am a grownup, and you, little girl, are no more than a drug addict. So if you want somewhere to stay, then you had best knock your crap off, 'cause your mother sure as hell don't want you."

As soon as she was done speaking, I slammed down the phone.

The thought that Mom didn't want me around hurt. I thought someone had just torn my heart out and stomped all over it. I knew I was a big disappointment for my mom, but I would never have thought she felt like that. I thought about going to her and asking her, but I couldn't handle it if she had said it was true. I wanted to cry but wouldn't allow myself. That's what made up my mind about going to Arizona.

I waited all the next day for Dad to call. Each time the phone rang, I jumped to answer it. But it was either Pete or Sue or someone for my aunt or uncle. When Pete called, he knew something was wrong.

"Sally, what's going on with you? This past week, you've been acting different. What's going on?"

I knew I had to tell him, but I wanted to wait until after I talked to my dad. I didn't know if he would change his mind or not, so I figured I should wait until he called.

"Pete, I can't tell you right now. But I promise you I will call you later and tell you what's going on. All right?"

He agreed, but I could tell he didn't like me keeping secrets from him.

That night, after I had put the kids to bed, the phone rang. I just knew it was Dad.

"Hello," I said into the receiver.

"Well, how is my girl today?"

"I didn't think you were going to call. You waited long enough." I laughed.

"It's cheaper if I call you at night."

We talked for a little before he brought up about me going down there to live. I was so scared he wouldn't bring it up. I thought if he didn't bring it up, then he really didn't want me down there.

"Have you thought about coming down here to live with me? If you don't want to, you don't have to. I want you to come only if you really want to."

He sounded like he was doubtful I was going to go.

"Yeah, I've thought about it a lot. And, yes, I will come down there to live. Maybe we can have a father-daughter relationship yet."

"I hope we can."

We talked about when I would come down. We planned it for after the holidays. He said that most likely all the seats would be taken right now, with the holidays right around the corner.

After hanging up, I called Pete to tell him. It wasn't the easiest thing I would do, but it had to be done.

"Pete, I have something to tell you that you won't like very much."

I hesitated. I really didn't want to tell him. My knees were shaking and so were my hands. I felt a cold sweat break out.

"I don't like the sound in your voice, Sally. What's going on?"

I just blurted it out to get it over with.

"I'm leaving to go to Arizona."

There was silence on the other end.

"Pete, are you still there?"

After a few moments, he finally said something.

"Why are you going to Arizona? And who are you going with?"

He sounded like he was going to cry.

"I've been talking to my dad for the last week, and he wants me to come out there."

"After all he's done, you're still going to live with him?"

"Pete, you do understand why I want to go, don't you?"

I wanted him to believe that it wasn't because of him.

"No, Sally, I don't understand. He left you, what, over six years ago, and you never heard from him until now, and he wants you to go live with him? Why?"

"Pete, he wants to get to know me. That's why. And, yes, it's been a long time. But I want to get to know him, too. He says he don't drink no more, so why not?"

"I think you're making a big mistake, Sally."

"If you want to fight with someone, Pete, then find someone else. I wanted you to know; that's why I called."

"No, Sally, you wanted to tear my heart out, and that's all you called for."

He slammed the phone down. All I heard was a click. He was upset, and I couldn't really blame him. I cried after he hung up, but I figured it was for the best that we broke up now. Neither of us said it, but we didn't have to.

Christmas vacation started, and I was going to go to Mom's. She was going to come and pick me up, so I had everything ready. It was snowing and blowing outside, so I thought it was Mom calling when the phone rang.

"Hello." My voice sounded deeper because I just knew it was her calling me to tell me the roads were too bad.

"Hi, Sally. How are you doing?" It was Pete.

"I'm fine. And you?"

It was dumb playing this little game like we had just met.

"I'm OK. I just heard from Sue that you were going to your mom's for your vacation."

"Yeah, I am."

I didn't know what to say to him anymore. I missed him. I missed having him call me every day.

"Look, Sally. I called to wish you a Merry Christmas. I didn't think you would be around after I talked to Sue. I wanted to give you a quick call."

I thought for sure I was going to cry. He sounded so depressed and alone. I wished I didn't have to hurt him like that.

"Thanks. I'm leaving sometime this afternoon. Whenever Mom gets here. I don't know when I will be back. But I have to come back to get my stuff, so I'll give you a call then."

"Yeah. OK. Look, Sally, I'm not going to say I'm glad you're leaving, because I'm not. If I had my way about it, you wouldn't be going nowhere. But since you are going, I want you to know I still love you, and I always will."

"I love you too, Pete. But this is something I have to do. I'll miss you and think about you all the time. And I hope the best for you. Take care of yourself."

A few moments later, I hung up the phone. I was really going to miss him. But I was thinking that going to Mom's for Christmas was the best thing.

Mom came and got me an hour later. I was thrilled to be getting out of there for a while. I wanted to be back in my old town. I wanted to see all my old friends before I went to Arizona. I wanted to tell them all goodbye.

Getting back to Mom's was not what I had expected. I thought everyone would be happy to see me before I left. But they all seemed like it was no big deal. Even Mom was distant from me. The words my aunt had said to me kept running through my head: "Your mother doesn't even want you." I thought she was right. I just stayed in my sister's bedroom for the first couple of days.

I hardly talked to anyone, so I figured I would get out of the house for a while. I headed to the arcade, hoping my friends would be there. But when I walked in only a few people were there. I went up to Dawn, one of the girls I used to hang with, and talked to her. I found out everyone was either away at relatives' houses or they had to stick around their houses 'cause they had company coming.

I talked to Dawn for some time, but she had to get home because she was going away. After she left, I couldn't believe how much things had changed while I had been gone. Every time I came home for a couple of days, there was no one around. It seemed as if they were all getting their heads together.

I stuck around for a while, then I went home. It was too cold to be walking around. Going home, I spotted a familiar car in the driveway. I stopped in my tracks. Snow was coming down lightly, and when I walked into the house, I had little snowflakes covering my hair and shoulders.

"Hey, Sally, someone stopped by to say hello," my younger sister said as she met me at the door. She was smiling from ear to ear.

"Kay, you had better wipe that silly little smile off your face before I do it for you," I told her jokingly.

She laughed and ran into the living room. I followed right behind her, and he was sitting on the couch like he lived there.

"Hi, Tom. What are you doing here?"

I tried to sound casual, but my heart was beating a mile a minute.

"Hey, Sally. I heard you were supposed to be home for the holidays, so I thought I'd just drop by with Al while he was visiting your sister and say hi." He smiled.

I sat down in the chair opposite him. I wanted to be as far away as I could be at the moment.

Neither of us said anything else. We were all watching a James Bond movie on TV. I really wasn't in the mood to watch TV. I kept glancing at Tom. He would always be perfect to me. I would choose him over Pete any day, but he would never know I even existed, except as a friend. I started comparing him to Pete.

Tom was dark-haired and had a bigger build. He was the first guy I ever allowed to take over my heart and remain there. He made me feel nervous all the time he was around, but he always shut me out.

I knew Pete was sweet and kind. He knew how to make me laugh and have fun without using drugs or alcohol. He knew when I needed space, and he would give it to me without a fight. And he never shut me out. So why would I want someone like Tom when I could have someone like Pete?

I shook my head and got up to go to bed. I told everyone good night.

I didn't see Tom during the rest of the time I was at Mom's. I didn't go out much. Christmas came and went. It was a fun-filled day for everyone. After opening my gifts, I sat back and watched everyone else. I wanted to be a part of that family more than anything, but I thought it was too late to even try. Until that day, I hadn't realized how I had built a shell around myself and kept everyone away.

CHAPTER 6

No one talked about me going to my dad's to live until the day I was to go back to my aunt's house to get the rest of my things. I was in the bedroom looking around. It was supposed to be my two sisters' and my room, but there was nothing of mine laying around, and I felt that room never belonged to me. Everything that was mine had been taken down, and God only knew what had happened to it. I was so lost in thought that I didn't hear my baby sister walk into the room. I jumped when she spoke.

"Do you ever miss this room, Sally?"

I looked at her for a second before lying to her.

"No, Kay, I don't miss this room. I'm glad I can leave all this behind me."

If she had known me well enough, she would have known I was lying because I didn't look her in the eye, which usually meant I was lying.

"I made you something so you wouldn't forget about me."

She handed me a little package. I opened it and saw it was a picture in a cardboard frame of her.

"Thanks. I'll put it by my bed when I get down there."

She made me want to cry.

"Sally, do you really want to go down there and live? I mean, you know how Dad was. I can't remember everything, but I can remember some of the beatings. Plus what everyone has told me."

I wasn't sure if that was the real reason she didn't want me to go.

"Kay, I've talked to Dad on the phone, and he is not the same person he was when he left us six years ago. Don't worry. I'll write you when I can."

We talked for a while. Then it was time for me to go. I thought she was crying when she walked away. She was the only one who even told me goodbye.

I had my things packed in no time at my aunt's. I was feeling restless. I called Pete when I got there, but I couldn't let my heart into the conversation. He kept telling me over and over how much he loved me and would miss me. I was glad to be off the phone with him. All the emotional strain was getting to me.

When it was time to leave for the airport the following morning, I really didn't want to go. If Mom would have told me I could go back to her house, I would never have gone to the airport. But she didn't say anything to me, and I couldn't say anything to her. I thought that if she wanted me to stay, she would have said something, but she didn't. The ride to the airport seemed too fast, even though it was a two- to three-hour ride. I sat in the back seat looking out the window. I wanted to tell Mom forget it and take me home, but I couldn't.

After we had got my ticket and were waiting for the boarding call, Mom sat on one side of the aisle, and I sat on the other. When my plane was ready to board, I was one of the first to get up to get on.

"Mom, you take care and give everyone a hug for me."

I sounded all choked up. I was barely able to keep the tears at bay.

"You take care, Sally, and make sure you write, no matter what. I love you."

I thought I saw a tear, but she turned away so fast, I couldn't tell. I quickly turned away and got onto the plane. Once I was seated, I burst out crying. My aunt was right; she didn't want me. If she did, she would never have let me board that plane.

I didn't know how long the plane ride was, but it was dark when I landed. I was nervous about seeing Dad for the first time in six years. Coming off the plane, I was afraid I wouldn't recognize him. But I was wrong; he hadn't changed much since the last time I saw him. I walked up to him slowly, unsure of what to do.

"Boy, look at my girl. You have sure grown up."

He was talking a mile a minute, never letting me talk at first. I hadn't realized he was with somebody until he turned around and spoke to a woman. I looked her up and down. She was skinny, with dark hair, and looked meaner than a rattlesnake.

"Sally, I want you to meet your stepmother."

I looked at him like he had lost his mind. I wasn't expecting him to have a girlfriend, let alone a wife. She held her hand out to me to shake it, but I wouldn't. Instead, I glared at her like she was some disgusting thing.

"I've heard a lot about you, Sally."

I didn't even like the way she talked.

"That's funny, 'cause I didn't even know you existed."

She glared at me. I could see the disgust in her face.

"That was going to be a surprise for you, Sally."

I couldn't believe he didn't tell me about her. All I could do was let it go for now. But if I was right, this woman and I were not going to get along very well.

The ride to Dad's wasn't very long. But it was long enough for me to find out what Dad was like right off the bat.

"Sally, I know you must be pretty tired after your trip, but before we get home, I'm going to tell you the rules you will follow while you're living with Nancy and Me."

I knew he was going to lay down the rules, but I thought he would wait for me to unwind from the trip. I sat there listening to all he said.

"Now, first of all, of course, you will not go out with any boys, and you will not be allowed no boyfriends. If a boy calls the house, you will be in deep trouble. You will go nowhere without telling one of us. There will be no friends over. You will not, I repeat, will not be allowed near the arcade. You will do your own laundry, clean your own room, and help Nancy with the housework."

I looked at him like he had to be out of his mind. I was going to be in a prison. I was better off staying at my aunt's. But he wasn't done yet.

"You will stay in school. There will be no smoking, so if you have some on you, you had best not let me find them."

He was strict, that was for damn sure.

When we finally got to the house, I was tired out. All I wanted to do was crawl into bed and not come out for a week. I carried my stuff in and put it in the room that was going to be mine. The first thing I noticed was that the door to the room had no lock.

"Dad, can I have a lock on my door?"

He snapped back at me. I couldn't believe this was the same man I had talked to on the phone. He was sitting at the table with a beer in his hand.

"Hell, no, you will not have a lock on your room. You will never have a lock on it as long as you live with me, so don't ask again."

I just walked away. Why had he changed. Was he only being nice on the phone just to get me down there or what? I didn't understand why he was like that.

The next day, I was enrolled in school. It wasn't a bad school. I really kind of liked it. If Dad would have been honest with me from the beginning, though, I would not have come. I couldn't make any friends, 'cause I was afraid Dad would get mad. He was always drinking, and it seemed like when he was drunk, he was the worst. So when kids tried to be my friends, I shunned them.

I wanted to go home. I felt lonely and unloved. I wanted to be back around Pete and the three kids. At least I felt loved then. But I couldn't just go home without a damn good reason. And that day came sooner than I thought.

I had been down there for less than two weeks when the first fight broke out. I had gone over to the neighbor lady's house. No one knew it, but I went over there to have coffee and smoke my cigarettes. She was a good lady, and I liked her a lot. She understood me. I hadn't realized I was over there for so long, and I told her I had to be going.

I walked in the door and should have known Nancy would be there to greet me.

"Where the hell have you been, young lady?"

I hated that woman more than I hated anybody. She knew how to get to me.

"I don't think that's any of your business, or I would tell you."

"Let me tell you something, little girl, and you had better listen real well. I am going to be your worst nightmare. I can make your life here hell. So if you want to be your daddy's little girl, you had better watch your step while living around me."

I looked at her like she was crazy.

"Lady, I don't know what you are talking about, but I think you are crazy and need some serious help."

I began to walk away, but she wasn't done with me just yet.

"No, Sally, you will need the help. See, all I have to do is tell your dad that you're whoring around or whatever I want to tell him, and he will believe me."

She smiled like she had just got away with something.

"Listen here, you old bitch . . . ."

That was all I got to say 'cause Dad came storming into the house. His face was beet red, and I could tell he was madder than a hornet.

"How dare you talk to your stepmother that way. Who the hell do you think you are? Let me tell you, you are nothing but a cheap-ass whore that uses drugs and alcohol. That's all you are."

He started hitting me and telling me no one in his house was going to act like some hussy off the streets. He didn't care where he hit me. He mostly got me in the arms and sides. I blocked my face so he couldn't hit me there, but he still managed to get in a couple of blows. He gave me one good shove that landed me in the living room on my backside. I jumped up and ran into my room. I stood over in a corner waiting for him to come in. I must have waited there for almost an hour. But he never came into my room. I began to cry and shake all over. I was scared to death.

When I realized he wasn't going to come in after me, I threw myself on the bed and cried. I wanted to go home where I belonged. It wasn't so much the beating that hurt. It hurt but not nearly as much as what he had said. I used to love my dad more than anything. but now I hated him more than I hated life itself.

Later that night, I was still in my room and lying in the dark. I didn't want to look at the bruises forming on my arms or sides. So I stayed in there in the dark. The door opened and then shut. I didn't move. I thought that if I faked I was asleep, he would go away. I knew it was him because Nancy hated me too much to even bother to come and see if I was all right. He started talking to me as if he knew I was awake.

"Sally, I am so sorry. I don't know why I got so damn carried away. Hell, I don't even know why I do a lot of things."

He kept talking, and I blocked him out. I knew he was sorry, and I also knew it would happen again. But I didn't know when. It was just like when I was younger; he wouldn't be happy unless he could hit someone.

Things went well for the following week. I stayed to myself. Dad let me alone for the first few days, but then tried to joke around with me. I wanted to scream at him to stay away from me. But I was too afraid another beating would come out of it. I wrote to Mom, but I couldn't tell her or anyone about the beating and what he had said. It hurt too much to think about it, so I put it in the back of my mind. The last time he would ever hit me again came sooner than I thought it would.

My uncle came over one night. He was one of the family I couldn't remember. I said hello to him but wanted to go to my room. Dad didn't want me to.

"Sally, go over and give your uncle a hug and kiss."

I couldn't believe he asked me to do that. I didn't even know the man. Sure, he was nice and all, but I still didn't trust him. By the look on Dad's face, I knew I had no choice. I leaned over my uncle and gave him a quick kiss on the cheek and a quick hug. He pulled me down and had me sit on his lap.

"See, I won't hurt you. I'm not a bad person."

He joked with me, something he did a lot, and I took to him right away. He made me feel comfortable being around him. He was the father figure I dreamed about. My aunt was real sweet, too. I liked them both. I remember thinking I would have liked to have lived with them. Dad must have read my mind.

"Don't even think about it, young lady," he said, looking at me.

I just kind of looked at him. After my aunt and uncle left, I sat on the floor and was playing Atari. I was in a good mood. I was thinking that maybe some time I would be able to go over and visit them. But my dad changed my mind for me real quick, I got a hit in the back of the head I turned around.

Without thinking, I said, "What the hell did I do now?"

My face went pure white. I couldn't catch my mistake before it was made.

"You rotten little whore. I told you before that you were not going to act like no whore in my house, and I meant it."

He started hitting me. He beat me so badly that night, I couldn't believe the bruises weren't worse than they appeared. I hurt all over, but my arms and sides again got the brunt of it all.

But he made it worse when he thought what he did about my uncle and me. He was crazy and disgusting. How could he have thought that about me? I knew then how low an opinion of me he had. That's when I made up my mind I was going to get the hell out of there. I didn't care how.

The next morning I woke up late. I took a quick shower because I wanted to catch Dad before he left. When I walked out to the living room, he was sitting on the couch with his head in his hands. He looked up at me.

"Sally, sit down here on the couch beside me."

I didn't want to, so I sat on the arm instead.

"I am so sorry, Sally. I never meant to hurt you that way, and I said a lot of things I didn't mean. I'm not sure why I did or said those things."

He sat there not looking at me. I think he truly was sorry, but there was not going to be another chance. I couldn't handle anything more.

"I called the airport this morning, so that you could go home to your mother if you want to."

I could not wipe the smile off my face. I was homeward bound. I didn't know when, but I was going home.

"I made the reservations for later this evening." He looked at me. He knew I wanted to go, and he wasn't going to stop me. He didn't say anything after that, so I ran back into my room. I started throwing everything into boxes and suitcases. I didn't even bother to fold them. I kept thinking that the faster I got out of there, the faster I could get home.

That evening I was sitting at the airport. I felt bad for Dad in a way 'cause I thought he was a sick man and needed some help. I no longer hated him. I just felt an emptiness that I couldn't explain. My dreams about my father had been shattered. I wished he would have been a loving man so that I could have know what it was like to have a real father to do things with. But that would be something I would never know.

Just before I got onto the plane, Dad pulled me into his arms.

"I love you," he said in a low voice, "and I'm more sorry than I can ever say. If you ever need me, I'll be only a phone call away."

I couldn't hug him back. All I wanted was to get on that plane. When he let me go, I walked onto the plane without ever looking back.

I thought that would be the last time I ever saw my dad. I sat down and buckled myself in. How could I have been so dumb to think that he could ever love someone like me. He was right about one thing. I was nothing, and I would always be nothing.

CHAPTER 7

The plane ride back to Michigan seemed long. I wanted to get home as soon as possible so I could get away from all the hurt I was feeling. I wanted to put it all behind me. Finally, the plane was landing. I gathered the few things I had brought onto the plane and waited for the landing to be completed. I just hoped Mom would be as happy to see me as I was looking forward to seeing her.

As I was getting off the plane, I spotted Mom, standing with my aunt. I wanted to run to her and put my arms around her, but I held back. She noticed me and smiled. My spirits fell right then. I thought she would really be glad I came back, but I was wrong once again. I walked up to her and smiled.

"Hey, how's it going?" I didn't know what else to say. I felt like an idiot standing there with my mother and not talking.

"Let's go get your stuff so we can go home," she said and went back talking to my aunt. I didn't feel like I belonged anywhere. I walked a little behind them with my shoulders slumped.

Nothing had changed at Mom's. No one seemed to care if was there or not. I drew further away from them all. I started partying. I was out drinking and getting high every night. If there was a party, I was going. I didn't care whose it was. When I first got home, I went to school, but the more I partied, the less I went.

People used to call me one cold bitch. The kids' mothers hated to see them hanging with me. I had such a bad reputation, everyone's parents didn't trust me. People used to say I had no feelings about others. I fought with anyone and didn't care who got hurt in the process. I was lashing my anger out at everyone. Sometimes, I got knocked around pretty good, too. I hung with one of the toughest crowds.

But one day I snapped. I got up one morning and thought I would put in an appearance at school. That was a mistake. For a couple of days, I had been feeling fidgety. I didn't know why no matter how much drinking I did or how many drugs I took I couldn't stop feeling nervous. I couldn't stand still. I thought maybe if I went to school that would take my mind off of being so antsy.

I walked into school, and everyone was surprised to see me. People were coming at me from all directions. I thought I was suffocating. I broke out in a cold sweat and was going to be sick. I walked up to the teacher and leaned over his desk.

"Hey, look. I have to go to the bathroom, like, right now."

He just sat there looking at me. I picked up the side of his desk and slammed it down.

"Why the hell am I asking you if I could go to the bathroom? I'll go if I want to."

I started walking out the door and heard the teacher tell someone to go get the principal. I made my way down the steps and to the door. I was getting ready to go out when the principal came up behind me and put his hand on my shoulder. I turned around and glared at him.

"If you ever touch me again, I will kill you. Get your damn hand off of me."

He removed his hand slowly.

"Sally, you don't look so hot," he said. "Why don't you come to the office. I'll call your mother, and she can come pick you up."

I don't know why I went with him, but I did. After calming down about him putting his hand on my shoulder, I sat down. He sat at his desk.

"I know you're doing drugs, Sally, and I think you need to get some help."

That was the wrong thing to say to me. I jumped to my feet and shoved his desk over. I was surprised to see he could move as fast as he did. I started smashing everything I could get hold of. I didn't speak a word. He got out of the office and locked me in. That made me go berserk. I couldn't stand it; it made me feel caged in. Then, Mom was there. I hated her at that moment more than anything. I started screaming at her.

"Why are you here now? You're never there when I need you. Get the hell away from me and never come near me again."

I started to get a bad headache. I grabbed onto my head and screamed at everyone standing in the outer office.

"The first one of you that comes in, I will murder with my own two hands. I swear I will."

No one came into the office until three big men, real gorillas, came in. They had one hell of a fight on their hands, but they got me to the courthouse and cuffed my arms and legs to a chair. The pounding in my head was worse, and I couldn't take the pain. Some guy came in and talked to Mom first. Then he walked over to me.

"Hi, Sally. My name's Steve, and I'm here to help you. Can you tell me what's wrong? I would like to help."

I glared at him.

"The only thing you can do for me is let me go so I can get some medicine for my head. It hurts. But since you won't, there's not a whole lot you can do for me."

I spat in his face. Most people would have walked away and left me alone, but not this guy.

"Sally, I'm your ticket so you don't have to go to a detention center. I believe you need some serious help, but no detention center. So, come on. I'll help you if you help me."

I looked at him and then looked over at Mom. I hadn't noticed she had been crying. I felt bad, but my head felt worse.

"All right, I'll settle down, but you have to get me something to stop the pain. I feel like I'm going to be sick."

He talked to me for a few seconds, then went and got me some pills for my head.

I went before a judge, but I couldn't remember what he said, no matter how hard I tried to focus on him. The next thing I knew, I was put in a police car and taken to a mental institution.

I hated being locked up. The only thing that kept me going were the pinball machines in the game room. I was in there for two weeks, long enough to dry out. I was told I had had a nervous breakdown, but because I wouldn't talk about my problems, they couldn't determine exactly what the problem was. They said most of my problems had to do with drugs and alcohol. That's what I was using to cope with whatever was wrong with me.

When it was time for me to leave, a man came up to me to talk about my release.

"Sally, I'm going to release you today, but I cannot release you to your mother. I have read your file, and I don't think it would be wise to send you there. I'm recommending you get some counseling after your release. From your charts, I see that since you've dried out, you haven't once gone haywire on us, so to speak. But I believe that between the drugs and your emotional status, that's what caused you to have a breakdown."

"If I can't go home, where am I going to live?" He hadn't said where I would be going.

"I have talked to your mother, and she has suggested you go and live at your aunt's house. Your Aunt Kim's house. She said she thought you had done a lot better over there than you had anywhere else."

He talked for a little bit about me going back to drugs and drinking. Then he had me sign some papers and said I would be released as soon as someone came and got me.

Later that afternoon, Mom came and got me. My aunt was with her. I already had my belongings packed and ready to go before they got there, so I could leave as soon as they came.

When I got back to the house with my aunt, the three kids swarmed all over me. They seemed so happy I was back. I felt better than I had in weeks.

The next day, I went to school as my aunt and uncle thought I was going to do. But I had other plans. I was going to call Pete once I was settled back in at my aunt's house, but I figured I needed to see him in person. That way, if he had another girl, I could go get high with one of his buddies.

I got off the bus at school, walked right into the building and out the other door. I walked up to Pete's house and noticed that both his parents' cars were gone. I was afraid that if they would have been there, they might have turned me in to the school I was ditching. I knocked on the door and hoped he would be home. I saw him before he saw me. He opened the door and stared at me like I was some sort of stranger.

"Hello, Pete."

He just stood there with a look of surprise on his face. I smiled, hoping that would bring him around.

"What are you doing here?"

The smile on my face disappeared quickly.

"Well, I thought I would surprise you and come over here and let you know I was back in town. But I can see it was a mistake."

I turned around, ready to go, when he stopped me.

"Where are you going?"

He sounded like he was puzzled.

"Well, I'm not going to stay anywhere I'm not welcome."

"Get in here. I was just surprised you showed up at my front door, that's all. The last time I knew where you were in Arizona with your dad."

I went into his house and sat on the couch.

"I was only down there for three weeks, and I came back home to Mom's.

I told him the whole story. I told him about Dad and all he had done and about partying too much and having my breakdown.

"Damn, girl. You've been through hell for the last couple of months. And your dad, what a . . . "

I cut him off before he said too much.

"Look, I learned my lesson about Dad. I don't hate him, though. I think I have enough reason to, but I don't. Just leave him out of it, OK? He's still my dad, and I don't want to hear anything bad about him."

"Who all knows about what your father did?"

He was standing by the couch looking at me.

"No one but you, and I want it kept like that. I don't want no one to tell me they told me so."

That's when I thought he might have a girlfriend.

"Pete, I have to ask you something, and I want you to tell me the truth. Do you have another girl?"

He sat down beside me and took my hand.

"Sally, I don't have anyone else."

I was so happy he didn't. We spent the rest of the day together. I felt so relieved to have everything off my chest. It felt good to talk about all the hurt and anger that had been bottled up for so long. Two months seemed like a lifetime to carry all that on my shoulders.

CHAPTER 8

Things were going all uphill. I didn't even mind watching the kids. My aunt started letting Pete come to the house. I did as I was asked to do, with no fights. I didn't think anything was going to go wrong. At least up until the end of May, when I got a phone call from Pete.

"Sally, I have something to tell you. And you won't like it much." He sounded like he was depressed or something.

'What's going on, Pete?"

"Things had been going so good that I didn't want to spoil it. And with you having your breakdown, I didn't want to get you going again. But now, I have to tell you. Today I went to court on something that I did while you were gone. And now I have to go to a Teen Challenge down in Missouri for the next thirteen months."

I was so dumbfounded that I didn't know what to say. I thought I knew everything about Pete, but I guess there were a few things he chose not to tell me.

"What the hell did you do? And why in the hell didn't you tell me sooner?"

I was mad as hell.

"It's not important what I did, and I couldn't tell you when you first came back."

I think I was more hurt than anything because I thought he trusted me like I trusted him.

We got into a bad argument that day. I ended up slamming the phone down on him. I couldn't get over that he hadn't told me from the start. My aunt was home that day, so I went outside and sat down

45

on the big tractor tire. I wanted to cry or scream or something, but I couldn't do anything. Instead, I sat there looking up at the sky.

"Sally, are you all right?"

I hadn't heard my aunt come out and walk up behind me.

"Yeah. I'm fine."

I didn't look at her. I thought maybe she would go away, but instead she sat down beside me.

"Sally, I heard you arguing with Pete. What happened?"

This was the first time in the whole time I lived there that she had ever asked me what was wrong. Without looking at her, I told her about Pete. I was shocked at myself for telling her. I never told her any of my problems. She made me look at her.

"You know he's right. You were not in a very stable condition when you came out of the hospital. You may think you were, but if something would have set you off, then it's most likely you would have gone back to the way you were. And as for him not telling you, maybe he didn't want to hurt you. Think about that, Sally, before you start getting all worked up."

She got up and walked away without giving me a chance to speak.

I sat out on that tractor tire for more than an hour thinking about what she had said. Maybe she was right. Maybe I wasn't all that stable when I first came out. I didn't know, but I couldn't let things go on like this between Pete and me.

I called Pete, and we worked things out as best we could. He still wouldn't tell me what he did. But that didn't seem to matter anymore. When he told me when he was leaving, nothing seemed to matter. He was due to leave in one week. Hanging up the phone, I went to my room and cried my eyes out. I knew now what he must have gone through when I left.

That week went too fast. He called me every night, no matter what. And then one night, he called to see if I could go to his last dance. I asked my aunt and uncle, and to my surprise, they said I could go. But they would pick me up when it was over.

That Friday night was hard. We danced to all the slow songs and just held onto each other. This would be my last time seeing him for more than a year. He was my everything, and he was leaving me.

I got to talk to Pete only once more that weekend before he left. I cried a lot after he was gone. I couldn't eat or sleep. I was lost without him. When my fourteenth birthday rolled around, I couldn't have cared less. I got what I had wanted for so long, but it no longer mattered.

My aunt and uncle went and got my gift for me. I took it upstairs and put it in a corner. The guitar was beautiful, but I no longer wanted to learn to play it. I always had dreamed of playing a love song for Pete, but now that he was gone, I had no desire to even learn.

Things went downhill then. I no longer cared about what my Aunt Kim and Uncle Dave had to say anymore. All I wanted was for them to leave me alone. We were always screaming and fighting. I couldn't stand being around her any longer. Then, one day, we got into our worst fight. I think I scared her that day.

We were standing in the living room yelling at each other. She made the mistake of putting her hand on my arm.

"Bitch, don't you ever put your hand on me ever again. I'd rather see your blood than your ugly face."

She took her hands off me.

"You just got your ticket home, kid."

And I did. I was moving out of her house the next weekend. Mom asked me what had happened.

"Mom, it's like this. I am not someone's slave. I don't think I should have to watch her kids all the time and clean her house."

Mom agreed with me, to my surprise.

At first things went pretty well at Mom's. We seemed to get along a lot better. I was talking to Tom and being his friend. But then we agreed to go on a date. It was my first date since Pete left. I still missed him and thought about him all the time. But it had been over a month since I had last heard from him, so I put him in the back of my mind. I still had his picture by my bed, so I never really could forget about him.

Mom somehow found out I was going out with Tom. She cornered me in the kitchen.

"Sally, I heard you were going out with Tom. Is it true?"

I couldn't tell if she was upset or not.

"And what if I am? Are you going to tell me I can't?"

I was waiting for her to tell me to stay away from him 'cause he was too old for me, but she kept her voice calm and cool.

"I think he is too old for you. And I think you should go out with someone more your age. If I told you that I wouldn't allow you to go out with him, you'd do it anyway. Am I right?"

"Yeah, I would and you know it."

I was not angry at her. She only spoke how she felt.

"See, it would do me no good to tell you that you can't. I'm going to leave this one up to you."

She filled her coffee cup and walked away. I thought for sure she was going to yell or something. But she didn't.

I wasn't drinking or partying anymore. I was trying to make amends with Mom. I was really trying, and so was Mom. That meant a lot to me. I loved my mother very much, but I never learned how to show her. I was not one to tell someone I loved them very often. To me, those words were just words. Anyone could say those words, but did they mean them?

The days went by quickly, and my date with Tom came around. I took special care in getting ready for him that night. I did my hair just perfect and put on my makeup just right. When I looked in the mirror, I couldn't believe it was the same person. I liked to wear jeans with holes in the knees and a T-shirt. That said me. But that night I put on a pair of black jeans with a button-down shirt and a vest and wore my penny loafers. I looked real good.

And when Tom picked me up, he met me at the door. We both were dressed very much alike. He had the same taste in clothes as I did. I thought we made a perfect couple.

We went out and got some wine and beer. We drove up to the pier. While the other couple we were with got out and walked the pier, Tom and I sat in the car. We talked about school and what I had done while living at my aunt's. I was taking a drink of beer, when he surprised me by asking me a question I was not prepared for.

"When you were living at your aunt's, did you have a steady boyfriend?"

After choking on my beer, I looked at him.

"Yes, Tom. I did."

What else could I say to him. What a subject to bring up at that moment! The pain of Pete's leaving was slowly going away, and I hated when his name was brought up outside of my house.

"You know, most girls would try and lie their way out of it. But you, you just come straight out and tell how it is. Why are you so different, Sal?"

"I don't know why I'm straightforward most of the time, Tom. Don't get me wrong. If I think I am in deep trouble, I will try and lie my way out of it." I laughed and took another swig of beer.

"Do you miss him?"

"Sometimes. I was crushed when he left. He helped me get through some hard times. He always believed in me. He was special."

"You know, it's going to be hard to find someone to play second best."

"There is no second best. I hope that when I marry, it will be for a lifetime. I don't want to be like my mother and father. Especially my dad."

Before we said anymore, the other couple came back to the car. The girl was sweet. She used to go out with my older brother, and even though they broke up, I still liked her.

"Hey, guys. Now it's our time for the car. We gave you guys an hour," she said, laughing.

Tom and I got out of the car and walked the pier.

"You know, no matter where I go I hope I could some day live by the water. It's so peaceful," I said.

I stood by the rail. Tom came up beside me and took my hand. His was much bigger than mine and warm. Neither of us said anything else the whole time we were standing there. I looked at him and saw he was lost in thought, so I didn't say anything.

Later that night, when Tom thought it was time I should be getting home, we sat in the back seat. I was pretty tipsy, but I knew what I was doing. We made out all the way to my house. He kissed me good night and left. I thought it was the start of something.

That night, all I thought about was Tom and how wonderful he was. I could barely sleep, I was so hyped up about my date. Finally, after laying there long enough, I fell asleep.

When I woke up the next morning, I was on cloud nine. Mom saw how happy I was and sat down on the other side of the table from me. She smiled at me.

"Your date must have gone real well for you last night."

"It did. He's the most wonderful guy in the world, Mom. He has always been my first love. I think I might let my heart take back over."

I was just as surprised as Mom when I said that.

"Don't get your hopes up, Sally. You're bound to get hurt again. Don't use Tom to get over Pete."

"You know, Mom, I thought my heart belonged to Pete. But he never made me feel the way Tom did. The only thing different is I gave my trust to Pete and not Tom."

"That should tell you something right there, Sally. I'm not trying to tell you what you should do. But I think you had better be careful."

"I appreciate what you told me, Mom. I really do. But I don't think Tom would hurt me."

She just smiled, and I went on my way. I called Sheila and asked her if she would take me out to Tom's. She told me she would be over in an hour.

Sheila and I talked about the night before all the way out to Tom's. I was so happy, I couldn't stop smiling. When we pulled into Tom's driveway, he was outside cleaning his car. I got out of the car and walked up to him. He smiled at me, but that was all. My smile was slowly fading from my face.

"Well, you told me to drop by today. So here I am. What are you going to do today?"

I tried to get him to take a minute and talk to me, but he didn't seem interested anymore. That hurt a lot, more than I was willing to admit.

"I'm really sorry, Sally, but Dad has asked me to so some things for him."

It was like he was trying to get rid of me. I thought that was OK, 'cause never again would I feel the same for him. He hurt me too much, and I walked away without looking back and went home.

Tom couldn't even look at me that day. Why? I had no idea. But it hurt. I chose to put it all in the back of my mind and go on. I never told Mom about what had happened. She had warned me, but I didn't listen.

CHAPTER 9

I started going out with other guys and drinking a lot. I did more drinking than I did anything else. I didn't really do many drugs, but the drinking was becoming a big problem for me. I didn't realize it until my little sister brought it to my attention.

She was the second person who made me realize I had a problem and what that problem could do to me. The first had been a friend. After I had left a party, a girl had been raped by some out-of-towners. But that didn't stop me from partying. Then my sister brought it up.

"Sally, Mom says you're going to be just like Dad, the way that you drink and all."

I didn't get a chance to say anything to her because she walked away. But I had not thought about it like that. I didn't want to be like Dad. He was a very cruel man, and I did not want to be compared to him.

I knew I needed some help, but I couldn't ask for it. I knew I had to, but that was asking a lot of me. It meant I would have to swallow my pride and go to Mom. I didn't have the nerve at first. But after a couple of days, I went to her. I waited until everyone else was in bed. I sat in a chair across the room from her.

"Mom, this isn't going to be easy for me, but I have to ask you for a favor."

She looked at me but didn't say anything. When I hesitated, however, she spoke up.

"I can't read your mind, Sally. What do you need?"

She wasn't being sarcastic or anything. Her voice was low, but I could tell she was curious.

"I need some help. I can't stop drinking. I don't think the drug use is that bad, but other people tell me differently."

I think I floored her. She sat there with her mouth hanging open.

"Sally, each time I help you, you always go back to the way you were. Are you going to try and stay clean this time?"

"Mom, I'm not going to sit here and tell you I promise. All I can tell you is I will try. I can't make a promise I don't know if I can keep."

"Then tell me why you want help, if you can't promise you won't go back again."

"Hey, look. If you want to help me, that's fine. But I won't sit here and have you criticizing me. I said I would try and I will."

"I'll help you, Sally, but you have to try. I don't mean for you to go get drunk when things are not going your way. Or if something hurts you. That's not the way to go about it. You have to learn to start talking to people. But you don't want to. You think everyone is going to turn away or stab you in the back."

I couldn't stand for someone to sit there and tell me the truth. But she had agreed to help. I didn't know how at the time, but she said she would let me know.

Less than a week later, I was admitted into a drug rehab program for eighteen days, after which I would be released. I thought it would be easy. Boy, did I have something to learn.

The first week was the hardest. I went through the headaches, the vomiting, and the mood swings. I couldn't stand to have anyone around me. I thought someone should have come in and just shhot me to get the pain over and done with.

After that first week, I was OK. I started feeling better. I even got out to meet the rest of the patients. Everyone I met was pretty cool. A lot of them had the same problem I had: not being able to deal with the pressure that comes from home. Some of them had lost loved ones and couldn't handle it. Others had their own reasons. The place was neat. In the morning we had to exercise before getting breakfast. We had one session of counseling in the morning and one in the afternoon. I wouldn't talk in the sessions, but I sure was interested in the others in the group.

By the time it was my last day, I was proud of myself. I had set a goal and completed it. I still had to make it through one more night, but I didn't think anything would go wrong. At about four in the afternoon, I was in the TV room when Kenny, one of the guys who was about my age, came in. He sat down beside me and put his hand on my leg.

"What the hell are you doing?" I yelled. "Get your hand off of me." I hated when guys thought they could touch anyone they wanted.

"I have something I want to ask you," he said. "I'm leaving here tonight. I'm going to go to see some friends of mine, and I thought maybe you would want to go."

I looked at him and couldn't believe he had asked me. I felt a little thrilled about it. For some reason, I loved being on the run. It was the excitement I liked. The more he talked, the more convinced I became that I would go with him. He was no one special, but he did know how to excite someone.

That night, we had some guy fake he was freaking out, and we went out the door unnoticed. I couldn't believe I actually left with him. All I had was one more night, and then I would have been able to go home. But, stupid me, I liked the excitement too much.

We hitched a ride to his friends' house, which was three hours away. Right away, we got a ride that took us all the way to where we wanted to go.

Once we got there, I was welcomed like I was some long lost friend. We all sat around talking and getting to know each other. But then Joe, the guy that lived there, brought out a bag of pills. Everyone started hooting. I sat there watching them take four apiece before he brought the bag over to me.

"No, Joe. I don't think so." I pushed the bag away.

"Oh, come on. It's not going to kill you. Lighten up and have some fun." I looked at everyone, and they all were watching me. I finally gave in and took only three.

"What are these?" I asked.

"Just say they are guaranteed to give you the buzz of your life," Joe said.

The first one was white, the second blue, and the third yellow. I threw them all in my mouth at the same time and swallowed them. I should have looked them over a little bit more carefully, because the next thing I knew, it was morning, and I couldn't remember what had happened the night before. I got up off the couch and went into the tiny kitchen. One of the girls, Rosemary, was having coffee.

"Hey, Rosey. What was that stuff I took last night? I can't remember what the hell went on after it kicked in. I've got one helluva headache this morning."

She was watching me and laughing.

"Don't worry about it. But you were funny last night. We let out the tarantula, and damn girl, I thought you were going to have a heart attack on us."

I shook my head and went to get Kenny up.

Everything seemed to go in slow motion for the next couple of hours. First the cops came to the door, looking for me and Kenny. Rosemary told them that neither of us had been there, so they left. Later on that evening, they came back. We knew they were watching the place, but we didn't think they would come back. As soon as we realized it was the cops, Kenny and I went to the back of the place and climbed up into an alcove.

I heard the cops looking all around. I was scared. When we climbed into that alcove, I saw pot plants galore. Plus there was a bag of stuff in the corner. I couldn't tell what it was, but I guessed it was more drugs. When I heard the door to the alcove open, I thought for sure we were busted. I held my breath until the door closed again. I guessed that the cop had not seen the ladder that would have led him to us. Joe hollered up to us when they left, and we climbed down not knowing what to expect.

"You guys are lucky, especially you, Sally," Rosey said as we walked into the living room. "They don't want you, really. All they want is Kenny."

She didn't say why they were after Kenny; she said she didn't know. I thought she just didn't want to tell me. I no longer cared. I just wanted to go home. They had enough drugs to send us all to jail, and that was one place I did not want to go.

We sat around talking about what we should do; we didn't know what to do at first. When Joe spoke up, it sounded like the best idea any of them had.

"Kenny, I know you don't want to hear this, but I think you should give yourself up to the cops. They'll catch you sooner or later, and when they do catch you, it will only be worse."

Kenny thought about it and said Joe was right.

"And, Sally, you can call your mom. Hopefully, she can come and get you before you get into too much trouble."

Kenny turned himself in to the cops who were watching the place, and I called Mom. I could tell she was upset, but she said she would come and get me. I gave her the directions, and she was there four hours later.

She was alone when she came. On the trip back, neither of us said a word. I felt bad for hurting her, but there was nothing I could do now to take it back.

Mom never asked me about that situation. I guess she was used to me doing stupid things. I wanted her to scream and yell at me or something. I didn't like her acting like nothing had happened. So I did as she did: pretended that nothing had happened. But I promised myself I would stay away from all the hard drugs. I didn't want anything to do with pills or coke or anything like that. Pot was all right; I knew I couldn't stop smoking that.

CHAPTER 10

I quit all the hard partying and started staying home. I quit hanging around most of the people from the arcade and kept to myself. I took long walks when things seemed to go wrong. I even let my little sister hang with me sometime. I still raised hell at times, but not like I had.

Then, Darren came into my life. He was OK. I liked him. He was funny and very shy. I think it was his shyness that attracted me to him. But some of my friends thought I shouldn't date a Mexican. They told me I should stick to my own kind. That didn't go over well with me. I never cared about someone's skin color, and I wasn't going to start now.

I went out with Darren and found he was a lot of fun to be with. I may not have felt like I did when I was with Pete or Tom, but I found him interesting. He always had me home at a decent hour, and our good night kiss didn't go beyond that for the first two months. He was different. He wasn't going out with me just to have sex, and that's one of the reasons I kept going out with him. The sex part didn't come up for a couple of months, and that was by my choice.

The trouble started when we started hanging with my girlfriend and her boyfriend. I noticed the difference in Darren when he was around them. He drank more and at times would pick a fight with me for no reason. I tried talking to him about it, but that didn't work.

"Darren, don't you think hanging with Paul's a bad idea? Whenever he's around, it seems like all we do is fight, and I'm getting sick and tired of it."

"I'm not going to stop hanging with him just because you don't like him, Sally. And we don't always fight when he's around. Sure, sometimes we drink too much, but who doesn't?"

I didn't want to hear any more, so I got out of his car, then leaned in the door.

"Well, then, you know what you can do with yourself and Paul."

I slammed the car door. I didn't care that I was on the other side of town from home. I walked home. By the time I got there, I was so mad, I think I could have spit fire. Mom noticed that something was wrong when I came walking through the door.

"What happened, Sally? Are you OK?" She was concerned. I could read it on her face.

"Yeah, Mom, it's all right." I took my shoes off and slouched in the chair.

"Come on, Sally. Don't clam up now. You've done so well since you come home, and I hate to see you mess it up now, especially over some boy."

I looked at her and thought she was one helluva lady to put up with a kid like me.

"I don't know, Mom. I guess it's just a lot of different things. Don't worry. I'm not going to do anything stupid. I just don't feel like talking right now, that's all."

She understood and let it alone. For now. But it didn't take long for her to find out what had happened.

"Sally, I'm proud you chose not to do drugs and drink. I know how hard it must have been to sit there and tell them you don't want to drink."

"Mom, it wasn't just that. I've tried to keep my act together, and to be honest, it was hard at times to say no. But I've been doing real well. But it was also making Darren and me fight all the time. I kept thinking back on Dad and you and how you guys always fought, and I didn't like it one bit."

"Well, I think Darren will be back. What are you going to say to him?"

"I don't know. It depends on him. I won't put up with his crap. That's for sure."

"Well, don't get suckered in."

She didn't tell me I shouldn't go out with him, but I could tell she didn't want me to if he came back around. I didn't know what I would do. I liked him a lot, but he had to change. That's all there was to it.

Mom was right: He was back a week later, standing on my doorstep wanting me to talk to him. I followed him out to his car, and we sat there.

"Do you want to go for a ride?" he asked.

"No, not yet. First, we have to talk about the problem." He knew what I was talking about.

"I'm sorry, Sally. I really am. I thought you liked drinking and partying."

I had never told him about my past problem. I didn't think it was important for him to know about it. But now I knew I was wrong to keep it from him.

"Darren, I do love to party. God, do I ever! But I had a problem with drinking, and now that I've quit, I don't want to start back up again. There's times when I give in, but not very often."

"You aren't that old to have had a problem like that. Hell, you're only, what, fourteen?"

"Yeah, but if you don't want to believe me, go in and ask my mom. She could tell you some stuff that I've done that most people haven't done when they're up there in age."

"Why didn't you tell me before?"

I explained my reasons, and he seemed to understand.

"Do you think we could go out again? Paul and I are still friends, but I won't do no more drinking while you're with me. Deal?"

I had to laugh. I didn't want him to give up his friends, just Paul. But since he wasn't willing to do that, I couldn't hold it against him. He gave me one thing: no more drinking.

We had no more problems after that. We got along real well. I couldn't have asked for anything to be any better. Mom and I got along, too. I even got along with the rest of my family. I was pretty contented until Darren came over one night with some bad news. He didn't even knock. He was always very polite when he was around my mom, so it kind of caught me off guard. It was the middle of November.

"Sally, we have to talk. Come on." He grabbed my hand and took me to my room.

"Damn, Darren. Nothing like being awful bold. Mom is sitting out there wondering what the hell you're thinking about right now."

"I've got a problem with my mom. She told me I can't see you any longer. She found out your age." He was holding me by my shoulders.

"So, she found out. Did you come here to break it off or what?" It bothered me, but I wanted to see if he was going to be a mama's boy or not.

"No. I'm not breaking it off. But I want you to come with me to Texas so we can be together always."

Leave home again? I didn't want to leave home. He was looking at me.

"What happened, Darren? You used to be so shy. You couldn't even look at me without blushing when I first met you. And now you want to run away?"

"We're good together, Sally. You know that. Paul is going with us."

We talked for a while, sitting there on my bed. I tried talking him out of it, but he would always come up with some reason why we should run off.

"You'll love Texas, Sally. It's warm and a lot bigger than this town. You'll be able to come and go any time you want. You won't have to ask someone for their permission. I can get a job and support us."

He convinced me to go with him, and we left that night. I thought it was funny he already had his stuff and Paul's stuff in the car. He was going to leave regardless of what I had to say on the matter.

CHAPTER 11

I didn't even leave Mom a note. I just packed a bag and went. We took the car to where Kenny and I had stayed and sold the car. We bought three bus tickets to Texas.

They were the longest days of my life. I could bathe only when we stopped at rest stops, and that just wasn't cutting it for me. I was tired and cranky. I wanted a hot shower and a soft bed. When we got to Dallas, we had to hitch a ride to Marble Falls. Paul told us it was about a four-hundred-mile hitch. It was going to take us a while to get there if we couldn't get some rides. At first, with the guys hitching, we got a lot of rides, but the closer we got to the smaller towns, the fewer rides we got.

"Darren, if we don't get a ride soon, we are going to fry out here in the hot sun," I said.

He didn't know what to do any more than I did. We were both in a strange place. Paul, on the other hand, knew exactly where we were. We were going to his brother's place, after all.

"Sally, if you think you could do any better, then you get out here and hitch us a ride," Paul said.

"I'll get us a ride a lot quicker than you would be able to. Darren, I'll be right back."

I grabbed his duffel bag and went into the store we were sitting in front of.

When I came back out, I had to laugh at Darren. I was wearing his gray shorts that were way too short and his gray half-shirt.

"I don't think you should be doing this, Sally. No, Sally. No way." He started walking toward me.

"Look, Darren. I'm hot and tired, and I want somewhere where I can get some good sleep. So you just go over there and sit down, and I will get us a ride."

He didn't like me standing out on the road the way I was dressed. But I didn't care. I wanted out of the hot sun, and I would do whatever I had to.

I was standing there for not even twenty minutes when a red, beat-up truck pulled up beside me. He asked me where we were heading, and I told him. He said he was heading there himself. We all rode with him all the way to where we were heading.

He dropped us off in front of a grocery store that Paul told us wasn't too far from his brother's place. We walked the rest of the way in silence. I was so damn tired I think I could have slept on the road if I had to. I couldn't wait to get there to bathe and get some decent sleep.

Once we got to Paul's brother's trailer home, he welcomed us and fed us. I took a hot shower and then cuddled up between Darren's legs and slept until noon the next day.

Darren and I were outside when Paul came walking up to us. I had a funny feeling in the pit of my stomach. I knew he was going to tell us something neither of us wanted to hear.

"Hey, guys. I have some bad news. My brother told me you guys can't stay here."

I had a feeling Paul had used us to get down here, and now that he had made it, he wanted us gone.

"That's all right. I had a feeling this was going to happen," Darren said.

I just looked at him. He must have thought the same thing I did. After Paul left, he turned to me and smiled.

"I've got an uncle that lives on the other side of Dallas," he said. "I knew he was using us, so I already talked to my uncle. He told me that if Paul did do this to us, then all we had to do was call him, and he would come and get us."

I smiled and gave him a big hug.

"I should have known you wouldn't let us take to the streets as a way of living."

We walked back into the trailer and got our things. We didn't say much to any of them. We just walked out and went back the way we had come the day before, back to the grocery store. Darren called his uncle from there. His uncle said he would be there in the next couple of hours.

We waited at the park across the street. I missed being home, but I sure as hell didn't miss the cold. I kept thinking about Mom and how worried she must be. Not knowing where I was or even if I was alive. This was really the first time I had been gone for a week without letting her know where I was and whether I was all right.

When the uncle finally showed up, I couldn't wait to get out of the heat. Even in the shade, it was hot. The uncle hugged Darren like he hadn't seen him in a long time. I was introduced to him, and he smiled at me. He was kind to me, but I was a little shy round him for some reason. I couldn't believe it; I was not shy around people that often.

Darren was happy to be with his family. He was contented. I couldn't break his heart by telling him his aunt didn't like me from the start. At first, everyone was supposed to share all of the cooking and cleaning, but before long, all the chores were on my shoulders. I did most of everything around there. Feeding and cleaning up after twelve people was hard work, but I thought there was nothing I could do about it. I was the only white girl around, and a lot of Mexicans didn't like me being there.

Darren was working ten to twelve hours a day, working on houses. He was the only one who really seemed to care. I looked forward each night to his coming home.

I though Darren and I knew each other pretty well. But it seemed I didn't know him half as much as I thought I did. We had gone Christmas shopping down at the local store. I was looking in the makeup department, and he was just down the aisle from me. I had picked up some eye shadow and was going to ask him if he thought his cousin would like it, but my words caught in my throat.

"Darren, what are you doing?" He was stuffing his pockets with stuff. I couldn't believe he was taking that kind of risk. He knew the cops knew where I was, but I was told they couldn't do anything unless

I did something wrong. If I got busted, I was going to be put in the detention center for a while.

"I'm not spending all my money on gifts, Sally. Put this in your pocket, and then we'll go and pay for the rest of the stuff."

We walked up to the cash register. I was scared to death. We paid for the other things, then walked out of the store. I hit him, and he laughed.

"Hold on. I forgot something."

He walked back into the store. If I had been smart, I would have taken off. I felt something was wrong. The next thing I knew, a guy came out of the store and put his hand on my shoulder. I knew then Darren had set me up.

I let the guy take me to the office. Of course, he was there. He couldn't look me in the eye. If he had wanted me gone, all he would have had to do was say so. I would have got home one way or the other.

I never got a chance to talk to him. Before I knew it, I was handcuffed and taken to jail. At first, I was hurt; then I became angry. Darren was lucky I couldn't get to him. I wanted to tear his dark head right off his shoulders and just rip him apart. After I was booked at the jail, I was taken to the juvenile center. It wasn't a bad place, but I wouldn't have wanted to go back.

I was there for a couple of weeks. I spent Christmas there, which wasn't bad. One of the Dallas Cowboys football players came to visit everyone. I wasn't interested in him. I stayed to the side, not caring if he was there or not. He introduced himself to everyone, but I didn't care who he was, so I walked away and went to my cell. He wasn't my family, so I didn't care who he was.

When New Year's Day came, I didn't think I would ever be heading back to Michigan. But the next day, I was put on a plane and was heading home. I may not have been going back to Mom's, but I would be closer.

The plane landed in Flint, where I was picked up by the authorities and taken to the juvenile center. I was to be there until my caseworker could find me a home to live in. I hated the center with a passion. There was one girl in particular I couldn't stand.

When I arrived at the center, I attracted one boy's interest. He was the boy this girl really liked. My first day there, she came up to me and got right in my face. That was the wrong thing to do. No one got in my face without having a fight.

"I'm telling you, bitch, you had better stay away from my guy," she said. "You are nothing but a little whore. the way you came in here walking like you are all it. Well, you're not."

I reached up and grabbed her fingers and twisted them backward.

"Don't ever put your fingers in my face ever again. You may not have them next time."

That's when the boy that the girl was interested in came up and told me to let her go.

"Come on, you don't want to have to go into the lockdown already. Do you? Give it a rest; she's not worth it."

I let the girl go and sat down on the couch to watch TV. I thought she might try and jump me from behind, so I sat by a wall where I could see her at all times.

The girl left me alone, except for making some smart remarks. As long as she didn't try to hit me, then I couldn't have cared less what she said.

I was in the center for only about a week before my caseworker came to get me. He didn't like me any more than I liked him.

"Sally, you're going to go to a shelter home for the next couple of months. And as soon as there's an opening in the home for girls down by Detroit, you'll be transferred there. If you screw up just one time, you'll live to regret it. Do you understand me?"

I hated this guy.

I agreed to do whatever it took to get me out of there. I hated to be in lockdown. I hated being locked up, period.

"All right. But just remember: One mistake and you're all done. I don't care what it is."

I just rolled my eyes and turned away. He signed all the papers, and less than an hour later, I was in the car, taking in the scenery. I didn't want to talk to this guy any more than I wanted to be in his car.

"I think you'll like it with this family. There's a teenage boy around

65

your age, and they have a two-year-old with them."

He kept talking on and on, as if I cared. I didn't pay attention to him after a while. I started wondering if we were ever going to get there. Just as I was about to ask him, he pulled onto a dirt road. Then after about the fourth mile, he turned into a driveway. There were two trailers, one in front and one in the back.

As soon as I stepped out of the car, I noticed a man and a woman coming out of the trailer in front. I was surprised to see they weren't as old as I thought they'd be. They came walking up to the car.

"You must be Sally," the woman said. "I was wondering if you were going to come or not."

She put her arm around my shoulder. Without being cruel, I pulled away. I lagged back a step so I could follow behind them. She showed me where my room was and then went out to talk to my caseworker.

I was putting my things away when she came back into my room. I looked up at her, expecting her to lay into me about the rules around there. But she didn't do it the way everyone else had.

"Sally, when you get through putting your things away, will you come on out to the kitchen so that we may be able to talk? Do you drink coffee?"

"Yes, I drink coffee, and yes, as soon as I'm done here, I'll be out."

She left, and I shut the door. After I put everything away, I sat down on the bed. For the first time in a while, I was thinking about Pete and what he would say if he knew all I had done. I also put his picture out on my dresser. I couldn't believe after all this time I still had his picture. I knew I had to get out to the kitchen, but I wanted to hold off for as long as I could. She called my name, so I knew my time was up.

I walked out to the kitchen and was surprised to see that not only had she made coffee, but she also had cake on plates. This lady sure was trying to be nice, I thought. I sat down on the other side from her, and she pushed one of the plates in front of me.

"I hope you like chocolate. It's one of my favorites. There's cream and sugar there for your coffee, too."

At the time, I drank my coffee black. I didn't have anything to say to her, so I sat there in silence.

"I want to be your friend, Sally, not your enemy. I think you and I can become friends if you let us."

"I don't need anyone as friends. I have all the friends I need back home." I said it with a bored tone, but she knew I meant it.

"I'm sorry you feel that way. We might as well get the rules out of the way. First of all, you cannot date. You can roam all over the woods or go down to the beach if you like, but you have to tell someone where you're going at all times. We supply your cigarettes and clothing as you need them. You can use the phone anytime you want, as long as its local. And knowing you, you most likely have friends around here, too. Before you say anything, I was told all about you. That's how I know."

"Is there anything else?" I asked.

"Yes. I would appreciate it if you would not cuss while Tina is around. She's the two-year-old who has been with us since she was a baby. That's all."

I finished my coffee and cake and went to my room without another word.

I closed the door so no one could look in. I was only lying on the bed, staring at the ceiling, but at that time I needed some time alone. I thought when the knock sounded on my door, it was Mary. I told her to come in. I didn't bother to look at her.

"Sally, is that really you?"

I looked over and saw that Jake was standing in the door.

"Jake, what the hell are you doing here?"

I jumped off the bed and gave him a big hug.

"I'm glad to see you, too. Man, it's been a while. You were the one that was coming! I was told Sally was coming, but I never thought it would be you." He laughed.

"Yeah, they told me there was a teenager that was staying here, but all I was told was that you were a boy."

He sat on the bed, and we started catching up on old times. He used to go out with a friend of mine, and when they broke up, he said things really started going downhill. His mother abused him, and that was why he was there.

"Well, I'm glad it's you here instead of some geek," I said, laughing.

We talked for the next couple of hours. I was so glad he was there, glad it was someone I knew.

But as the days started to go by, I needed someone besides Jake to talk to. So, one day I decided to be brave and call Tom. He wasn't there when I called, so I left my number for him to call me back when he had a chance. I didn't think he would, but I needed to hear his voice.

I started liking Mary and Jim, her husband. They were really cool. We all played cards or watched TV. It depended on everyone's moods, I guess. I walked the woods and the beach every day. I thought of all the things that had gone on in my life, and I couldn't believe I had made such a mess of it.

First, my father left. Then, we moved, and my mother went out with some guy I couldn't stand. Then, we moved into town, and I hung out with the wrong crowd and got into drugs and alcohol. I went to my aunt's to live, then went to my dad's in Arizona, came back to Mom's, went to drug rehab, ran away with some guy, came home, then ran away to Texas, went into a detention center in Dallas, was sent back to Michigan to another detention center, and now I was sitting in this shelter home.

What a mess! I had hated my life, and now that I wanted to make things right, I couldn't. I wasn't allowed to go to Mom's for a while, and that really bothered me. I hadn't seen her in two months, and I wanted to see her and my family.

CHAPTER 12

When I came back from my walk one day, the phone was ringing as I walked in the door. I picked it up as I was walking past it.

"Hello."

"Sally, is that you?" It was Tom.

"Yep. The one and only," I said, smartly.

"Hey, girl, it's good to hear your voice. I would've called sooner, but I was out in the fields with Dad."

We talked for some time that night and each night after that. Either I called him or he called me. I loved to hear his voice, so soft and sexy. I could listen to it all night.

I was due to leave for the girls home in the beginning of March. I had found out in the middle of February that there would be an opening for me then.

The closer it came, the more depressed I got. I would never be able to talk to Tom again, and that bothered me more than anything else. He could tell something was wrong.

"Sally, what the hell is going on with you? You're so quiet. Normally, you're talking a mile a minute, but lately you've been really quiet."

He was getting to know me more and more. I didn't know how to handle it, so I lied to him.

"Nothing, really. I guess I'm just really tired, that's all."

"You know, you don't make a good liar, especially when you're talking to me."

I laughed. Only he would know.

"All right. How about if I tell you the truth? Hmmm?"

For some reason, it was harder for me to tell him anything that went beyond friendship. I would do anything for him. I thought he knew that.

"Well, the closer the day comes that I'll be leaving is just putting me down in the dumps. That's all."

"Well, just think of all the people who will still be here waiting for you to come home."

I wanted to ask him if he would be one of them, but his next words took all my breath from me.

"Oh. Guess what. I'll be leaving for Florida soon."

I was dumbfounded. I didn't want him to leave.

"Ah, Tom. I have to go. Mary's yelling for me."

He told me he would call me the next night, and we hung up. I went to my room and sat on my bed. It seemed to me like everyone I ever cared about always left me. I couldn't figure out why. I curled up into a ball and cried myself to sleep.

I don't know how long I had been asleep. Someone was shaking my arm, trying to get me up. I heard my name whispered. It was dark in my room.

"Sally, wake up. Come on. I want to talk to you."

It was Jake. He had never come into my room at night before.

"Jake, what do you want?"

I was still half asleep. What could he want to talk about at this time of night, I thought when I looked at the clock on the dresser. It was a little after one in the morning.

Well, you didn't get up for dinner, and I heard you crying when I walked past your door after you came in earlier. I just wanted to make sure you were all right."

"I'm OK. C'mon and sit down."

I sat up so he could sit by my feet. He sat down and put his hand right above my foot.

"Sally, I know you were upset with Tom when you got off the phone. The only time you get that lovesick look is when you're talking to him. I just can't believe you would waste your heart on someone like that, especially when there's a lot of guys out there who would love to have someone like you."

I knew he was talking about himself. I had to set him straight.

"Jake, I love Tom. You're the first person I've ever told that. I don't know why I do, but I do. I wish more than anything that I was older because he's all I ever want.

"I had an idea you had a real crush on me just by the way you act when I'm around other guys or when I'm talking to Tom. But I thought it would pass. I think of you as a brother. I don't want to be anything more than your friend."

I didn't want to hurt him, but he had to know I could never feel anything more for him.

"See, Sally, you're so different. Since you've been here, I've got to know a sensitive side to you. I always thought you were some cold-hearted bitch, but that's just an act you put on. You laugh when Tina does something stupid and tell her to try again, and I noticed that you can't stand to see people cry. You won't go to them, but you have to walk away; otherwise, you will cry right along with them."

I hadn't realized he watched me that closely. I hated that he was getting to know me so well.

"Look, Jake, if you ever tell a soul what you just told me, I will hate you for the rest of my life." I didn't want anyone to know me like that.

"Chill out. I won't tell no one. I promise. But why don't you give someone else a try? You might be interested in someone else." He was bound and determined.

"I've gone out with more guys than I care to admit to," I said, laughing.

"What about him?" He pointed to Pete's picture.

"He was someone that was special to me. I could never forget him. He taught me a lot about love."

We ended up talking way into the night. I felt sorry for him. He had no one who loved him. His father left him, and his mother abused him. He finally went to bed after kissing me on the cheek. I had a heck of a time falling asleep. I slept too long, and he came in and woke me up again.

I had a lot to think about regarding Tom over the next couple of days. I avoided his calls for a few days. Because he was leaving, I thought it would be better if I kept my distance from him from here on out. I loved him too much to get hurt again. After making my mind up, I called him.

"Sally, it's about time. I thought you were never going to call. I kept being told that you were busy or something." He sounded happy that I had finally called.

"Yeah. I have been."

"Well, I have something to ask you. But you have to listen and hear me out before you say anything."

I was puzzled by his tone but agreed to hear him out.

"I want you to go to Florida with me. I think I could make you happy. I'm leaving soon, and I don't want to leave you behind."

It was everything I had ever dreamed about. I could go away and be with him for always. But the thought of Darren popped into my mind.

"Why do you want me to go with you?" You could get anyone you want, so why me?" I wanted to hear him say he loved me.

"I don't know." He laughed but there was no humor in it.

"Then why are you asking me to go with you?" I wanted him to say it so bad I had to bite my lip.

"I guess you call it love."

That was all he said. He didn't come out an tell me he loved me. That hurt. He wanted me to go away with him, and I wanted to, but he wouldn't tell me what I wanted to hear. How could I leave with him if he really didn't love me? I thought he would do the same thing Darren had done, and I couldn't deal with it if he left me like that—set me up when he was done with me. This was one guy who could break me in two.

"Love? Do you even know what that is? You can't even tell me you love me. No, Tom. I don't think I will leave with you. Take care."

I hung up the phone, and before the tears could fall, I grabbed my coat and ran out the door.

I went to the beach and sat on the steps. It was February, so no one was around. I had the whole place to myself. "I love you, Tom," I said out loud, over and over. He would never hear me say those words. I would have given anything to take back what I had said and tell him I would go with him. But I wanted his love, and I didn't think he could ever love me.

After that day, the spark died in me. I no longer cared about anything. I had lost the one person I wanted. For me, the world could have ended right then, and I couldn't have cared less. I withdrew from everyone, even Jake. He tried to draw me out, but it never worked. I just wanted to be left alone and to forget that Tom ever existed. It was easier said than done. I thought about him when I woke up and when I went to sleep. How could I forget someone I had loved for three years? I didn't know how to get him out of my system, so I just bottled it all up inside. I no longer cared about anyone else, I would not do what anyone wanted me to do. I had the biggest case of attitude possible. It tore me up knowing that Tom was most likely gone by now. I took my torment out on everyone.

One night Jim and Mary had to go somewhere, and they left Jake, Tina, and me with a friend of theirs. He had ordered pizza, and we all were drinking straight shots and having a lot of fun. The booze made me forget about Tom for a time.

I had gone into the kitchen for another shot when the pain hit. It brought me to my knees, and I couldn't move without it hurting more. Jake came into the room and saw I was in pain.

"I'll call Jim and Mary," he said.

I watched him run from the room as the pain got worse. I screamed and cried for someone to help, but all I felt was someone's hands trying to comfort me by rubbing my back.

It didn't take long for Jim and Mary to get there. Mary squatted down in front of me and said, "Sally, where are you hurting?"

I pointed to where it hurt, and that's when she could tell I had been drinking. She could smell it.

"What the hell has she been drinking? Oh, never mind. Let's just get her to the hospital."

I was carried to the car and put in the back seat. They rushed me to the hospital as quickly as they could, but to me, they weren't moving fast enough.

Once I was at the hospital, and all of the IVs were in, all sorts of tests were done to find out what was wrong with me. Mom was called, and she was there with my shelter parents when the doctor came in to talk to us.

"We can't find what's wrong with your daughter," he said. "We've done a series of tests, and nothing has shown up. So, what we're going to do is wait until morning and see what happens."

Nobody in the room liked what he said, yet nobody said anything.

I was given pain killers all through the night, but I was still not doing so well. If I wasn't given the pain killers, I was in so much pain and I let them know it. The nurses were glad to be able to shut me up.

Mom came in the next afternoon when she got off work. Her face turned red when she looked at me.

"Hasn't the doctor come into see you yet?"

I shook my head, and she went marching down the hall. She came back into the room with the doctor. With my caseworker, shelter parents, and mother there, the doctor said something that upset everyone.

"I think what your daughter should have is a hysterectomy."

Once he said that, I looked at Mom. I knew what it was and that it meant I would never have any kids of my own. I didn't like the thought of that. I had always looked forward to someday having a couple of kids. Mom looked at me and started shaking her head.

"No, we will take her to another doctor first. She is too young to have one of them without a good enough reason. And you haven't given me one yet."

She was mad, and when my caseworker spoke up, that's when I think the doctor really listened.

"I'm with the Department of Social Services, and unless you give us a damn good reason why you would want to do this to such a young girl . . . ."

I don't think the doctor liked it very much, but he didn't have much of a choice. The next thing I knew, I was being prepped for surgery. Nurses were coming and going, and I was out before I was even out of the room.

When I came to, everyone except my caseworker was there. My main focus was on Mom. She looked at me and smiled.

"They found your appendix was ready to burst, so now there's nothing to worry about," she said. "And as soon as you can walk well enough to satisfy the doctor, you'll be getting out of here."

I was glad they found out what was wrong. I was scared it was something more serious.

The next morning, I started walking the halls—not very well, but I did my best. I was out of the hospital within a week. I was slightly bent over and in some pain whenever I tried to move too fast or when I stayed on my feet too long. But the doctor thought I was ready to leave. He told me I had to get plenty of rest and walk daily. In a way, though, I hated leaving the hospital because that would mean I wouldn't see Mom every day.

A couple of days after I had been back at Jim and Mary's, I was doing some cleaning. When my stomach started hurting, I quit and went into my room and lay on the bed. I hadn't been laying there long when Mary came in.

"Sally, I want you to get up and come out and do the dishes," she said.

I couldn't believe her.

"Kiss my rear end, woman," I responded. "I just laid down. I did your other crap for you, now you can do the rest."

That didn't go over very well.

"You will do as you're told, young lady. I won't stand here and listen to none of your nonsense. Do you hear me?" She was practically yelling.

"You're a crazy old bat, and a lazy one, at that. I'm not your damn maid, so do it yourself," I yelled back at her. I got up off the bed and pushed past her, grabbed my coat and went out the door.

I walked for more than a mile to get to the nearest phone so I could call Mom. I was pissed 'cause I didn't feel I should have to do all of the chores around there while Mary sat around watching TV. I called Mom and told her what had happened and let her know where I was. She said she was on her way to get me.

CHAPTER 13

I went back to Mom's until the following weekend, when I went to the girls home in Dearborn. It was pretty cool, and the people were nice. We went places such as the carnival and went out to eat. I went to Mom's on home visits every other weekend. I was doing well. In two months, I made up two years of schooling. Mom told me over and over how proud she was that I was doing so well. Things couldn't have been any better for me, up until Pete came home.

When I knew he was home, I called him from the home. He sounded a lot different. His voice was a lot deeper.

"Where are you, Sally? I've been home for a week, and no one knew where you had disappeared to. Sue said she thought she knew but wouldn't tell me."

I was surprised he had come home a week early.

"Well, today was the day you were due home, so that's why I waited till now to call." I told him where I was, and he was upset I had got into so much trouble.

"Look, Pete, I don't have that much time to talk, so I'll be home this weekend and maybe I'll see you then."

"All right. I'll see you this weekend. Don't forget."

I was too excited to forget. This was going to be the longest four days of my life.

When I went home that Friday night, I was so excited I could barely wait. Mom picked me up at the bus station like she always did, and we went out to eat, then headed for her house.

Mom had moved out of the city into a six-bedroom house in the country. It was big and a lot better. I liked it 'cause all of us kids had our own rooms. I took the smallest room 'cause I was there for only two days on the weekend.

That Friday night, I kept my sister up until almost morning. I was too nervous to sleep. In the morning, Mom was taking me to see Pete, and I couldn't wait. I slept for only an hour before the alarm went off. It didn't take me long to get up and get going. I was all ready to go even before Mom was up.

"Sally, when you go to see Pete, I want you to take your sister with you," Mom said. I didn't care if she came. I woke her up to tell her. She was glad to go. She wouldn't have to say in the house all day.

I was pacing the floor by the time Mom and Kay were ready to go. I thought it would take them forever. Mom kept telling me to calm down. She kept saying we were going to be leaving soon. When they were ready, I practically pushed them out the door before they could say they had something else they had to do.

When we reached town, I told Mom to drop us off at the corner on Main Street. I told her we could walk the remaining four blocks. I needed the extra time to get my nerves under control. My hands were shaking, and I was smoking one cigarette after another. A couple of times, I almost turned around and walked away. I didn't know if I was doing the right thing or not. But my sister kept pushing me along, telling me everything was going to be OK.

When we came around the corner to Pete's, I saw him doing something in his car. I saw him before he spotted me. I walked up to him slowly, feeling so unsure of myself. When I reached his car, I spoke up.

"Pete." I didn't know what else to say to him. He stood up by the car and shifted from foot to foot. I was staring at the ground, feeling real shy for some reason.

"Are you two going to stand here all day or are you going to hug? Come on. I'm not standing around all day." Leave it to Kay to speak up. Both Pete and I started laughing, and at the same time, he gave me a huge hug.

That was the only contact we had at first. But when we went for a walk, he held my hand. There was no kissing or anything. He wanted to talk first. We walked for a while, not really saying much, but when we came to a field a little way out of town, we decided it was as good a place as any to talk. Kay left us alone for a while so we could.

""I've got to know what happened, Sally, for my own peace of mind. I've heard so many rumors, you wouldn't believe them all." I felt bad for him, but I was thinking he deserved to hear the truth, and who better to tell him than me.

"Most of the rumors you heard are most likely true, Pete." Then I began telling him my story. I told him everything except about Tom. I left him out of it. Pete stayed a little ways away from me after I began telling him about everything. It was hard telling him 'cause I knew I was hurting him. But what else could I do? When I was done telling him, he looked at me.

"You honestly thought I wasn't coming back, even though I told you I was?" I think he was more angry that I hadn't taken him at his word.

"Look, Pete, I'm not the most trusting kind of person; you know that. So, if you want to hold all this against me, then go right ahead. I won't sit here and beg you to forgive me. I won't do that for nobody, and that means you, too." I got to my feet and looked over at my sister.

"Sally, it's not that I want you to beg me. I just don't understand why you did all that."

I wondered how I could make someone understand what I was going through if he had never gone through some of the things I had gone through.

"You'll just have to try and understand me, Pete. I don't know what else to tell you."

He sat there, trying, I thought, to decide what to do. I wasn't going to push him. I was the type of person who felt that if you liked me, you would take me for who I am.

"OK, Sally. I don't want to lose you again, so I guess I really don't have much of a choice but to put it all behind us and start over."

"But, Pete, if we argue, you can't just throw it in my face because of what I did." That was one thing I could never put up with. I hated for someone to condemn me for what I did in the past.

"All right."

After we got it all out in the open, we had a pretty good time. We laughed and joked, hugged and kissed and just had a damn good time. I think Kay was glad everything worked out. She liked Pete when she first met him. We tried to include her in having a good time, too. I was surprised to see Pete joking and laughing with her. No one liked most of my boyfriends, so this was different for me.

That night, for the first time, Pete and I slept together. He didn't want to at first, but with a little talking, I got him to give in. We were in my room and talked almost all night long. I forgot how good it felt to talk to someone.

The next day, it was hard to say goodbye to him. I was so scared I would never see him again. One day just wasn't enough to catch up on everything. I didn't want to go back to the girls home. No matter how well I was doing, I didn't care anymore. I wanted to be with Pete and nowhere else.

At first, when I went back to the home, I did what I had done every day. But after a while, it no longer mattered. I didn't want to go and eat or go do the same activities I already had done. All I wanted was to go home.

In June, one month after Pete had come home, I had finally had enough. I went and spent my time as I always did with Pete, but when Sunday came, I had other plans. Mom and my aunt took me to the bus station as usual.

"Mom, I don't need you to walk up with me anymore. I think I'm big enough to do it by myself now." I was a little harsher than I had been in months.

"That's OK, Sally. I like walking you up and telling you goodbye. I know you're big enough, but it's something I like doing."

"Well, I think I can do it myself." I got out of the car and slammed the door. I knew that by doing what I was going to do I was taking a big risk, but I didn't care. I could still remember what my caseworker had said to me when I first came to the girls home.

"Now, if you mess up here, Sally, you will regret it," he had said.

"You see, I know of a place I could put you, and believe me, you won't be coming out of there."

That put a little fear into me. I didn't know all of what he meant, but I didn't like it.

I looked back at Mom, and I didn't think she knew what to do at first. I went behind the bus so she couldn't see me going into the bus station. After the bus had gone and I thought Mom was gone, I walked out and stood there for a second. I had planned on hitching a ride back to Pete, but when I looked down the road, I saw Mom coming. I hurried back into the bus station and went into the bathroom.

I wasn't in there long when I heard the door open. I knew it had to be either my aunt or Mom. I put my feet up on the toilet so that when they looked under the doors, they wouldn't see me. I held on to my stuff, trying not to make a sound, but it was hard.

I sat there for a little bit longer after I heard the door shut. I sat down on the toilet, telling myself, Thank God, they didn't catch me. I wasn't going back to the girls home, not right now, anyway. When I came out of the bathroom and went back outside, who should be sitting there in the car but dear old Mom. I looked at her and shook my head.

"I'm not going back, Mom. Not this time. I'm going to go home to Pete, and there's nothing you can do to stop me. So don't even try." I was looking straight at her.

"Why, Sally? Don't you realize what could happen to you if you don't go back?"

"I really don't care much anymore." She couldn't change my mind, so she told me to get into the car. No one said anything to me all the way back home. Eventually, the car stopped in front of where my aunt worked.

Pete happened to be walking down the road when we pulled up. He looked at me, and I could tell that he was shocked to see me in the back of the car. I got out and went over to him.

"Sally, what's going on?" He looked from me to my mom and then to my aunt.

"Sally says she's not going back to the home. Maybe you can talk some sense into her before she regrets what she's doing." The longer Mom talked, the angrier I got.

"No one needs to talk some sense into me. I know exactly what I'm doing. So you can take a hike and just leave me alone for the rest of my life." I screamed at her. Pete took my arm and pulled me behind him.

"OK, Sally. Calm down. We'll go somewhere so we can talk." He looked at Mom and waited for her to nod her head.

"What do you have to do, wait for her to tell you what you should do?" I turned on him so fast that he didn't know what to expect.

"Calm your ass down, Sally. I don't need anyone's permission to do something, but there's something that you have to learn about and that something is called respect." Before I could say anything else, he grabbed onto my arm and pulled me away.

He took me to his house and up to his room. At first, I stood in the doorway, but he gently pulled me down onto the bed and sat beside me.

"I know you're mad as hell at me, Sally. But it doesn't help anything for you to stand there and argue with your mom. She's only doing what's best for you. She knows what could happen to you if your social worker finds out. And none of us want that. I love you, Sally, and there's nothing I wouldn't do for you. But, dammit, I don't want to have to wait for another three years before I see you again."

Three years in that godforsaken place I was told about is what I would get if I was busted again. I wouldn't be released until my eighteenth birthday.

"Pete, I know what could happen, but I'm not going back. I can't."

He sighed and sat with his head in his hands. After a while, he looked up at me with a slight smile.

"You know, you're as stubborn as a mule. I won't make you do something you don't want to do, but, Sally, you have to promise me that if you get busted and you get sent away, you won't blame me for it."

"I promise." I laughed and hugged him at the same time.

I didn't think he understood why I wouldn't go back. But this last visit home had done me in. When I had first arrived home that weekend, I had found out that my little brother and my little sister were going down to Dad's for the summer. I couldn't see my little sister going, or my brother. But my little sister couldn't handle the abuse if

81

Dad put her through the same thing he put me through. That really sent me off the deep end.

We spent the night at Pete's sister's apartment. Because both his sisters shared the place, we slept on the couch.

I couldn't sleep too well that night. Each time I almost went to sleep, I seemed to see the same thing over and over again: the angry faces of cops, coming to get me. They wanted to take me away for a very long time. Finally, when I was too tired to keep my eyes open any longer, I fell into a deep sleep.

When I woke up, it was after nine in the morning. I had only a little over five hours of sleep. I wanted to get ready and get the hell out of there as soon as we could. But Pete wasn't ready just yet.

"Come on, Sally. We have lots of time before we have to leave. Lighten up."

I had a bad feeling, and I didn't like it.

"Pete, I think we should get out of here. I'm serious, man." He laughed.

"You're just being paranoid, Sally. That's all. You know you're in big trouble if you're caught."

"Maybe you're right."

I sat back down on the couch. Pete went in and took a shower. When he was done, it was my turn. I kept thinking the police were coming with each passing moment. After I got out of the shower and got dressed, I went out to the kitchen where Pete was getting us something to eat. I told him I wasn't hungry; all I wanted was coffee. When we were done, we thought we would find somewhere else to stay. We were walking out the door when we spotted the cops pulling up.

"Oh shit, Pete, now what do we do?" He ran to the back door, looked out, then came back to me.

"There's cops in the back, too. Come on. We can go in the basement and hide out."

I followed him, not really knowing where we were going. Once we were in the basement, he told me to hide on top of some barrels that were stacked in the corner. I stayed there until I heard the police. I debated whether I should come out, but the thought of Pete going to jail terrified me.

"Sally, I know you're in there. Why don't you come out and make it easier for everyone?"

I climbed off the barrels and walked up to the cop.

"Here I am. Leave him out of it. He had nothing to do with it." I smiled at Pete when he came out of where he was hiding.

"Sally?"

Pete started saying something. I shook my head, and he knew I was telling him to shut up. I was walked out to the cop car, handcuffed, and put into the back seat. I waved goodbye to Pete as the car drove off to the station. There, I was strip searched and made to put on a uniform. Then I was shown to my cell.

The cell was bigger than the one in Texas. It had four beds, a shower, a toilet, a sink, and one big, long table. I was given some books to read, but there was no way I could sit and read one. My social worker was coming in the morning, and he wasn't going to be very happy with me. There had to be a way out of this. I started pacing the floor, trying to figure out what I could do, Then, it came to me that there was only one way I could do this. It had to work.

I slept well that night. I thought for sure my plan was going to work. For my sake, I prayed it would.

The next morning, I hurried and took my shower and was ready by the time my worker got there. When he walked in, I was ready. I was on my bunk, curled up in a ball.

"Sally, how are you doing this morning?"

I could barely answer him politely.

"I'm in here for something stupid, something I could have avoided." I hung my head. It was hard for me to keep a straight face when all I really wanted to do was laugh. My plan was going to work; I just knew it.

"What do you mean, Sally?" He was neither rude nor nice, just curious.

"I made a mistake. I should have gone back, but instead I went with my boyfriend. Come on, give me another chance. I swear it won't happen again. I promise. Come on, give me another chance?"

If he really knew me, he would have known it was all an act and nothing more. But he didn't know me that well, so he couldn't know whether I was putting him on or not. After he saw the tears, I knew I had him.

"All right, Sally. This is your last chance. If you screw up this time, you're out of here. Do you understand that?"

I was tickled 'cause I had pulled off the tears act.

"Yeah. I understand."

"Good. Now I'll go sign the paperwork, and then we'll be on our way. But, Sally, I mean it. Don't mess up again." He walked out the door, and I felt like dancing all over the cell. I didn't have much space to get around in, so it didn't take me long. It took a hell of a lot longer for my worker to get the paperwork done.

When we were finally on the road to the home, all I heard all the way was that this was my last chance. It irritated me for him to sit there and keep it up, but I was afraid that if I said anything, he would change his mind and take me to the other place. I sat there listening to all he had to say. I didn't like it, but I sat there saying yes to him all the way.

CHAPTER 14

When I got back to the girls home, I was no longer the only white girl in my dorm. Another white girl had come in the day before, and she was being teased as I walked into the dorm. I looked at her, and if we were on the street, I most likely would have teased her, too. But being in a place like this, you had to have some compassion for the girl. She looked so lost and alone that I felt sorry for her. Being away from the ones you loved was hard.

I still had my plan in mind, but when I met that girl, I thought I would include her. I was in my room, lying on my bed. I had trash duty that night, so I was waiting to go and do that. I wasn't expecting the attack that came when I wasn't looking.

"You rotten bitch."

I was pulled off the bed and got the hell beat out of me. When one of the women supervisors heard what was going on, she came running down the hall. As soon as everyone heard her coming, they all took off to their rooms. I had no idea what was going on or why they had done it, but at that moment, I didn't care. All I knew was I was in a lot of pain. I looked up at the woman who had come into my room.

"What happened in here? Who did this?" she asked as she helped me get up and took me out to the TV room. When I didn't answer her, she sat down with a towel and was drying off the blood. She asked again.

"Sally, who did this to you? You're not going to be in trouble. All you have to do is tell me so that we can get it straightened out and so it won't happen again."

I was no snitch on the streets, and I'd be damned if I was going to be one in there.

"No one. Don't worry about it."

She looked at me, then got up and walked out of the room. When she returned, she had all of the girls with her.

"I want every one of you to sit down, and you had better listen good. I don't know what has gone on here tonight, but whatever it was, this whole side of the dorm will be punished. Since Sally doesn't want to tell me who done this, would one of you prefer to?"

She looked at them all; they all hung their heads.

"All right. Since no one wants to tell, then in the morning, you all will know what your punishments will be." She told them all to go to their rooms and stay there. She got me some ice for my eye, and I went to my room with the other white girl coming right behind me.

Once I was in my room, I closed the door and told her to sit down. I sat in the chair beside the bed.

"All right, Rachel. This is what I'm going to do, and if you want to come, then you can. If you don't want to, you can't tell no one. Is that clear?" She nodded, so I went on.

"I've had some time to put this plan together, so I was glad I got trash duty tonight. Now, what I'm going to do is when I take the trash, I won't be coming back in here. I'm going to jump the fence and get the hell out of here. I'm going as far away from here as I can get. And this time I won't get caught."

"Yeah, but you know it's not safe on the streets after dark." She sounded like she wanted to go but didn't want to go in the dark.

"Look. I'm not going to dink around. If you want to be a chickenshit all your life, then so be it. But you'll find that living on the wild side is sorta fun. That is, as long as you don't get caught." I chuckled at her.

She agreed and wanted to go, so I went and asked if she could help me take the trash out. The dorm woman didn't think twice about it; she said OK when I told her there was a lot of trash.

When I told Rachel to get her personal stuff and put it in a trash bag, I thought she was a little scared about going.

"Sally, are you sure you want me to go with you? I mean, I won't get in the way?"

"I don't care if you come or not. It's up to you. But I'm going."
She didn't say anything else and went to get her things.

When it was time to go, I gathered the trash and mixed our bags in it. We threw the trash in the bins and took our bags. I threw off my nightgown. I had on a pair of jeans and a T-shirt under it. I tossed the nightgown into a bin and took off running, with Rachel trailing behind. I was glad she had done the same thing I had done with clothes under her nightgown, 'cause there was no way I was going to stand around and wait for her to change.

We ran to the fence, and I helped Rachel over the barbed wire. On the other side of the fence, there was a short stretch of trees and beyond that, a parking lot with some sort of building—apartments or something. We stayed right on the edge of the trees for some time. I wanted to make sure the cops were not looking for us in that area. Most people would have taken right off and got the hell out of there, but I figured they never would have guessed we would be just on the other side of the home. And I was right.

After we waited for a while, I went looking for a pay phone. I was going to call Pete so he would come and get me. I knew he would 'cause there was no way he would let me be on the streets for any length of time.

I didn't take us long to find a phone. There was one right around the building where the parking lot was. I called collect, and Pete accepted the call.

"Sally, where are you?"

"I'm on the run again, Pete. I need you to come and get me." I told him where I was and how to get there.

"Why did you run this time, Sally? My god, girl, you want to be locked up for a long time, don't you?

"Hey, Pete. I didn't call you so you could give me a hard time. I called for your help. But if you don't want to help, then that's just fine. I can make it on the streets just fine, too."

"Calm your voice down, Sally. I'll come and get you. But I just don't know what I'm going to do with you. You're one surprise after another. I think you enjoy this kinda stuff a little too much." He laughed and said he would be there as soon as he could. I didn't tell him about Rachel. I didn't know what he would say.

After a couple of hours that seemed like forever, he finally pulled up. I knew it was his mother's car. I was surprised to see she came with him with his brother-in-law. When I ran up to him and gave him a hug and a kiss, Rachel walked out. He looked up and saw her.

"Don't tell me she's with you. Please, Sally. You know, I'm taking on a lot with you, let alone her, too. Sally?"

I looked at him with a smile.

"I couldn't leave her 'cause of the way the girls treated her. They were mean." That's when he looked at my face.

"Who the hell beat you up?" He was mad.

"Oh, just a bunch of them tramps back there at the home. It's no big deal.. Let's just get out of here before the cops spot us."

We all climbed in the back seat and relaxed. Now that I knew I was safe, I felt like I hadn't slept in weeks.

"Sally, wake up. Come on. We're at my folks' house," I heard Pete saying as I woke up. We got our things and went into the house. Rachel, Pete, and I went to his room to talk.

After sitting on the bed, I asked him, "Pete, where do we go from here? You know we can't stay here 'cause the cops will be here first thing in the morning. That's how they caught me the last time." After I said that, I felt guilty 'cause Pete looked like I had just slugged him in the stomach.

"Sally, I'm sorry I didn't listen to you. I should have, but I didn't, so I know it was my fault for you getting picked up the last time. I just didn't know the cops would show up that soon."

"Don't worry about it, Pete. It's over and done with. So now we have to do something so that I don't get caught again. Do you have anything?"

Rachel sat in a corner of the room without saying anything. She seemed too shy around Pete because she didn't know him.

"Yeah. I do have someplace in mind," Pete said. "But that is if you're not afraid of the dark and woods." He was joking with me but being serious with Rachel.

"I'm not afraid of anything," Rachel told us. She was so nervous her leg was shaking.

"OK. This is what we're going to do. First of all, I have a tent in the garage, and I'll find something for her to sleep in. I hadn't planned on someone else coming, or I would have had it all ready by now. The only things I got around here was the stuff for you. So all we have to do is go to the garage and see what we can find."

We all went out to the garage in the middle of the night and looked for something we could use for Rachel. Pete found a tarp we could use. We headed out to the woods that belong to the parents of one of Pete's friends. When we got to this real nice clearing, Pete told us that's where we would be staying. It was a nice spot. It was all cleared out and looked like it was where people went camping all the time. The river was close, and I could hear it. It was peaceful and quiet. I liked it right off the bat. That's where I would stay for a while until I knew of somewhere better to go.

The following day, the cops showed up at Pete's early in the morning. I was right. Pete had got up early that morning and gone to the house. I was glad he did 'cause I didn't want them to link him to me.

>From then on, for a month, I lived in the woods. I took my baths in the river. Pete brought food out every day, and we cooked it over the fire. But it was lonely at times.

The more I got to know Rachel, the more I didn't like her. She didn't want to go to the river and get cleaned up. I couldn't handle being around someone who wouldn't keep herself clean. I really tried putting up with her, but I couldn't take much more. Maybe it was because her and Pete and a few friends were all I saw, and I wanted to be out doing something. I couldn't tell what it was.

I thought about how she must have felt being away from all her friends and family, but it was hard for me to even care after a while. Things got out of hand one night when I had to get out of the woods for a while. I couldn't stand to be cooped up anymore.

"Pete, you have got to get me out of these woods for a while. I know the risk I'll be taking, but I can't take too much more. We can go to the movies or drive-in or something. I don't care. Please."

He didn't like it, but he agreed to get me out for an hour or two. I didn't trust Rachel staying behind, so I asked her if she wanted to go. "Yeah, I'll go with ya. It might do me some good to get out of here for a while."

"All right," Pete said. "I'll call Joe and see if he wants to go out with her. This way you and I can be alone without someone feeling out of place." He had a point. Having Rachel around, I always thought I had to be careful 'cause I didn't want to make her feel any worse than she did already. It was hard telling what she might do.

That night, we all went out, Joe with Rachel and Pete and I. We went to the drive-in to see some space movie. We took Joe's truck, so he and Rachel sat in the front, and Pete and I sat in the back. We just lay back there, looking up at the sky and wishing on the stars.

After we were dropped off that night, Rachel started saying things that really bothered me. She was confused about Joe, and that wasn't good.

"Sally, I want to marry Joe. He is so sweet and caring. I think I love him. I want to go and see him."

I turned to her and said bluntly, "Rachel, just because you two had sex doesn't mean he loves you. And besides, how can you say you love him when you only met him tonight? Come on. Give me a break. I think you need some serious help if you think he's going to see you again."

"He wouldn't had had sex with me if he didn't like me," she said in a whining voice.

"Rachel, let me tell you a little bit about Joe. For one, the type of guy he is, he's not just for one girl. He likes to check them all out. It will be a long time before he's ready to settle down. He likes anyone that puts out."

In a way, I felt bad for her 'cause I think she truly thought he loved her or something.

"You're just jealous, Sally. You don't like it 'cause I found someone."

"What the hell do I have to be jealous for? I'm just telling you the facts, and I really don't give a damn if you like it or not. As far as I'm concerned, you can get your stinky ass out of here. I don't even know how he could do it with you. You smell too bad."

I was screaming at her. Pete had to grab onto me and pull me back. I was going to hit her like she had never been hit before.

"Let's go in the tent and calm down, Sally. Come on. Just leave her alone." He pulled me into the tent and let me scream about her. I couldn't understand how she could be so naïve. Even I wasn't that naïve."

The next morning, we all got up, and before I knew what she was doing, Rachel had got her stuff together and was walking down the path.

"Where do you think you're going?"

"To see Joe, and I'll show you how wrong you are about him."

I looked at Pete, and we took off after her. When we caught up, she didn't want to listen to either of us. So we watched her walk away. She had no idea how to get to Joe's, but I imagined that she was going to guess about how to get there.

We didn't know what to expect after that. Pete went to his house to see what he could find out. When he came back, he came the back way. He had Pat and Stan with him. I knew something was wrong as soon as I looked at him.

"Sally, hurry and get your stuff together. There's all sorts of cops up at the gravel pit, and they're heading this way. And guess who's with them?" I knew before he even said it. Rachel. I was petrified.

"Shit. Now what do we do?"

Pete was getting things into bags and loading up Pat and Stan's arms, telling them to take the stuff to the car.

"Sal, I brought the car, and we're going to get the hell out of here. Now, let's go, or you're going to be going away for a long time."

I hurried, and we went out the back way to where his buddies were waiting for us at his car. We all jumped in and took off like the devil was at our backsides. We dropped Pat and Stan off at a corner outside of town.

"I don't think it would be a good idea if we went into town," Pete said.

"I know, but I want to know what's going on. Come on. I'll slouch down in the seat so no one can tell that it's me." I needed to know what was happening.

Sure enough, there were cop cars all over out at the pit. I couldn't believe Rachel had gone to the cops. She was dumb for taking off in the first damn place. We didn't know what we were going to do, so we drove around for a while trying to figure out what we should do from here on out.

"Pete, why don't I go to one of my friends' houses until everything calms down. I just don't want to drag you down with me, that's all." He really wasn't thrilled with the idea, but what other choice did I have?

"I guess we have to. But it will only be for a week or two. Just long enough for me to figure out what to do. OK?"

So, I headed to my friend's house to see if I could stay there until the heat cooled down.

Staying there was all right, but I wasn't sure how long I could handle all the noise. I guess I had become so used to the quiet that I couldn't stand rowdiness. Things were going pretty well until the third day. I was sitting in the living room when one of the girls, the oldest one who lived there, came running into the house.

"Sally, the cops are on their way here. I just got done talking to them, and they want to talk to Debbie about whether she saw you in the past month or so. They questioned me, but I told them I hadn't talked to you in a long time."

It didn't take me long to run to the phone to call Pete.

"Pete, you have to come now. The police are on their way over here to talk to the girls. I know it will take you about forty-five minutes to get here. I'm going to split, and when you get here, if there's police out front, don't stop. Then, you come back, and the girls will let you know where I am. All right?" I had to talk fast because I wasn't sure just when the cops were going to show.

"You just be careful, and I'll be there before you know it."

We hung up, and I went back to the bedroom. I didn't know what to do. The cops knew all my hangouts. I was pacing the floor when Debbie walked through the door.

"What are you doing, Sally? You know the cops are on their way."

"Debbie, I don't know where to go. They know where I hang out. So now I don't know what I'm going to do."

She sat down on the bed and tried to figure out a place too, but she couldn't think of one, either.

"I know where I'll go. Down by the fairgrounds. I don't go there very often, only when the fair is going on. They'd never think of looking there."

"Yeah. Let's hurry and get your things together."

We put my stuff in a bag, and I took off out the back door. I waited at the fairgrounds until Pete came for me. To me, it felt like forever, but it really wasn't that long. I was waiting in one of the barns.

"I know what we're going to do," Pete said. "I thought about it all the way over here, and I think you might like the idea, too." He turned and smiled at me.

"We'll worry about that later. Let's just get the hell out of here."

He took off down back roads so he wouldn't be spotted by the cops. After driving for a while, he found a gravel pit and pulled into it.

"I want to take you to the Teen Challenge place where I was at. I think they could help you liked they helped me."

"Man, I don't know. What if they turn us in? Then what would we do?" I wasn't sure if I liked the idea or not.

"My guess is that they would help you and get our lives on track."

We talked for a while, and I finally gave in, but there was one problem.

"Pete, what are we going to do for money? We can't walk that far. We'd get busted for sure."

He thought for a second before he spoke again.

"What I'll do is go to my house tonight and take two blank checks out of Mom's checkbook. We won't write them for too much, just enough to get us through."

I agreed with him, but we would have to wait until dark.

Around 10 o'clock that night, we were out by his house. He went through the yard and into the house while I stayed outside. We didn't want to take the risk of me getting caught. He was in there for less than five minutes. We both ran to the car and took off, laughing all the way.

CHAPTER 15

Going to Missouri was a long ride. Pete wanted me to stay awake while he drove, but it got harder for me to keep my eyes open with each passing mile. He nudged me awake so he wouldn't fall asleep at the wheel. When he finally got too tired to drive any farther, we pulled into a rest area and slept. The closer we got, the more my nerves were straining. I was hoping they would help us where we were going, but I didn't have my hopes up any.

When we finally reached the Teen Challenge, I was scared to death. The place was back in the woods a little. The scenery was beautiful. There were quite a few buildings all around the place with a gravel pit off to one side. If I hadn't been so tired, I would have wanted to walk around the place and check things out. But right off the bat, we were taken into one of the buildings and fed. The people there didn't talk to me much; they mostly talked to Pete. They could tell I was awfully tired. One of the women counselors came up and asked me if I wanted to go and lie down.

"Do you mind, Pete? I don't think I will wake up until morning, so I'll see you later." I kissed him on the cheek and told him good night. He had warned me we wouldn't be able to stay in the same house together, I didn't like the idea about us being apart but there was nothing that I could do.

The people were all very nice. A woman took me to a room that was plain but nice. I didn't hesitate about lying on the bed. I wanted to see how good it felt it seemed like an eternity since I had slept in a nice warm comfortable bed. I would have liked to have snuggled next to Pete but I was contented to fall asleep in a comfortable bed.

When I got up the next morning, I went looking for Pete. I couldn't find him, so I waited for him at the car. People walked by and said "Hi" but kept walking. Pete finally came out of one of the buildings that I saw a lot of guys going in and coming out of. He walked up to me with a big smile.

"Good morning, babe. Did you sleep well last night?" He was in a very cheerful mood.

"Yeah. I slept real well last night. And by the look of you, so did you. But, Pete, you had better take me somewhere so that I can have a cigarette." I felt like I was going to come unglued on someone real soon if I didn't get some nicotene in my system real soon.He told me to get into the car, and he would take me down by the pit.

While we were there by the pit, I started getting a funny feeling in the pit of my stomach. When I looked out of the car window, I noticed a man standing off to one side, watching us.

"I don't like this, Pete. I think we should get the hell out of here now. I have a bad feeling in my gut." He laughed and shook his head.

"Quit worrying. You have to trust someone sooner or later. These people are pretty cool. They would never turn us in.Besides they dont even know that we are on the run." He was convinced the people were genuine, but I didn't like the way the guy was watching us. It was like he was afraid we would get out of his sight.

"Pete, something's going on." I was beginning to get really bad vibes.

"Sal, you know I would never let anything happen to you. I made that mistake once, and I'm not going to make it again."

I still wasn't convinced, but I had to take Pete's word for it 'cause I had no idea where I was. I didn't even know how to get out of the place.In my heart I knew that Pete was wrong. The people here may have helped him but in the pit of my stomach I just knew that something was about to happen.

When we came up from the pit, the guy walked behind the car. That's when I knew he was watching us for sure. But I couldn't say anything. Pete was enjoying being back with all of his friends. He parked the car, and we went into the building we had gone into the night before and got some breakfast.

We sat in there for a long time talking to people. I really wasn't interested in what they had to say. All they wanted to do was preach to me, and there was nothing I hated more. The people were only trying to help, But I still did not want to be preached to.

Later that afternoon as Pete and I were standing in the middle of the drive, I still had an uneasy feeling in my stomach. A white car pulled up, and I knew right away it was an unmarked cop car. I looked up at Pete, and he looked at me. I watched as a man got out of the car and walked toward us.

"I told you, Pete; we should have gotten out of here when we had the chance. But, no. You said it was because I didn't trust anyone. Well, now you see why." I was screaming at him. Then, the cop spoke.

"There's no escape, Sally. Every corner for miles around is blocked off. There's nowhere for you to go."

That's when I went wild. I started pounding on Pete's chest, telling him I hated him. He just wrapped his arms around me. He seemde so defeated it broke my heart. These people that he trusted just tore us apart again.

"Come on, Sally. Let's go," the cop said as he grabbed my arm and escorted me to his car and put me in. As I watched out the window I could see Pete and I could tell that he was crying. As I waved good-bye to him, I watched as he hung his head and I knew that he was hurting as badly as I was.

I was taken to the local juvenile center. I was angry because Pete had not listened to me. Now I was going to go back to Michigan and get stuck being put into a home that I would not be released from until I was eighteen years old. The more I thought about it, the more I was determined I would escape the center somehow.

When we reached the center, I was taken in and escorted to a little room off to my right. There I saw a woman sitting behind a desk. When she spotted me, she gave me a huge smile. I glared at her.

"I presume you're Sally. Well, my name's Kelly, and I'd like to get to know you a little. It looks like you could use a friend. Do you have anything you'd like to talk about?" She was smiling all the time, and that seemed to get on my nerves.

"Look, lady. I ain't new to the game, so cut the bull. I don't need no friend or anything with anyone from here." I was sounding very rude, I didn't care. I knew that she didn't really want to be my friend she just wanted to send me back to Michigan.

"Sally, I know your background. See, we knew you were in the Teen Challenge last night. You see, in fact, it was the Teen Challenge people that turned you guys in. We told them to keep an eye on you until we could get there. I called your caseworker last night, and he informed me you ran away from a girls home back there. I don't know the whole situation with you, but if you'll let us, we'd like to try and help."

When she finally shut up, I was madder than hell. I could feel my blood pressure damn near boil over. Help yeah right, there was no one that really wanted to help me.

"Look, lady, I know you have a cell here for me, so why not just save your breath and just show me where it is." I glared at her.

"Well, we've had it set up for you to be heading back home come Monday morning. You will stay here for the weekend and Monday some one will be here to pick you up. In the meen time why dont you just relax and maybe when you cool down a little then you might want someone to talk to."

"Listen lady I dont want to talk to anyone. Just show me where my cell is." She sighed and shook her head. Then she led me through a rec room where there were other kids watching t.v. I really didn't pay to much attention to them because what caught my eye was a glass door to my right that looked like a little fenced in court.

I had two days to plan on how I was going to get out of there.

She told me I had to take a shower and put on a blue uniform. I did as I was told, then went to my cell for the rest of the night. My dinner was brought to me by a girl who was also in the center. She was big for her age, a little younger than I was.

We weren't allowed to have anything but a book in our cells. I found out that the girl's name was Peggy, and the only other kid in there was a boy named Kevin. He was pretty cool, but I didn't trust either of them. All the girl could talk about was getting out so she could get laid. That was all she wanted.

I couldn't sleep very well that night. For one, Pete wasn't there and for another, I was trying to figure out how I was going to get out of there. I finally fell asleep; God only knows what time it was.

The next morning I awoke to someone calling my name from the door.

"Come on, Sally. It's time you got up and got some breakfast." I turned over and saw Kevin standing at my door.

"All right. I'm coming," I said as he walked away.

I got up and went to where the others were. I sat down, and sure enough, Peggy started in on how she wanted out. I ignored her and finished my breakfast and went outside to the gate. There was no grass, just a big court so all you could do was play basketball. The fence was just like the one I had gone over at the girls home, so I knew it wouldn't be hard to get out of there. But first, I had to plan it for the right time. There was no way I was going to go back to Michigan and get locked up for who knew how long. I knew it would be until I was eighteen, but I was afraid they would find somewhere else for me after that.

I went in and sat down on the couch. I had to get my mind off the situation. I was starting to get an awful headache. My nerves were strung out, and everything was getting to me. So I thought if I relaxed for a bit, my headache would go away.

Lunch came and went, and I was starting to get real antsy. I didn't want to watch anymore TV, and I didn't want to sit and read a book. I wanted out, and I had to do it before Monday.

I was sitting at the table later that afternoon when I heard someone knocking on the door. I didn't bother to look up 'cause I figured it was someone who worked there.

"Sally, you have a visitor." I looked up, and Pete was standing there with a huge grin. I jumped to my feet and was in his arms in no time flat. I was so happy to see him, I started crying.

"How did they—I mean, how did you get in to visit me? It's

supposed to be only family members allowed in." I don't think I made too much sense at the time, but I didn't care. He was there, and that was all that mattered.

"Calm down, girl. They let me visit you 'cause you don't have no family down here. I called this morning, and they had it arranged so I could come up." I took his hand and led him over to the table and sat down.

"Pete, you know they're planning on me going back to Michigan Monday morning. You know I can't go back there." I was whispering so the other two couldn't hear me.

"I know, Sally, but you knew the risk when you split the other place. Now, all we can do is deal with it the best way we can." He was trying to reason with me, but it wouldn't work.

"No, Pete. I'm not going back there. I'm splitting from here, and there's nothing you can do or say to stop me." I was too determined to listen to anything other than getting out of there.

"Dammit. What do you plan on doing now?" I could tell he really didn't want me to do anything stupid. When I told him what I planned on doing, he really got upset.

"And how did you think you were going to manage out there all alone, with no money or anything?"

"Look, Pete. I can take care of myself. You know that. There's ways I can do it, so don't worry about it. All right?" We stared at each other for a moment before he finally gave in to me.

"OK, Sally. I can tell you're pretty serious about this. So, what I want you to do is find out who's working tomorrow night and see if he's cool, and then I want you to sit tight until I get here tomorrow. Promise me you'll do that for me."

I promised, and when he left, I wanted to cry. The only thing that kept me intact that night was that he was coming back the following day. I did as he asked and went to the other two to find out what Pete told me to find out. I went first to Kevin because he has been there the longest.

"Kevin, do you know what the guy who's working tomorrow night is like? I mean, is he cool and all?" He looked at me kinda strange before he answered.

"Yeah, you would really like the guy that works tomorrow. He's one of the coolest. Why do you ask?"

I didn't want to tell him anything 'cause I didn't know if he would tell anyone or not. But I didn't have to say anything; he figured it out.

"You're breaking out of here, ain't you? I can tell by the way you're acting. That's why you want to know who's working tomorrow night, 'cause that's when you're going to do it!" It was more of a statement than anything. When I still didn't answer him, he was about to keep pushing the issue, but just then, Peggy came walking over.

"Whatcha two talking about?"

I looked at Kevin and shook my head, but he ignored me.

"Sally's planning on splitting out of here tomorrow night."

I hung my head 'cause that was one person I did not trust at all. I couldn't believe he told her. I looked at her, wondering what she was going to do and say.

"Are you really? If you go, can I go? You won't even know I'm around. I swear."

What was I supposed to say? If I told her no, she would most likely tell on me, and if I said yes, then I was taking on more than I could handle. I looked long and hard at her, but I really had no choice but to tell her she could go.

"If I take you with me, you have to stay out of my way. These people don't know it yet, but I think I might be pregnant. I'm not sure yet, but I'm almost positive. So you had best stay out of my way."

She was happy to be going. And I thought I was taking on one of the biggest mistakes of my life.

"Oh, and Kevin, if you want to come, you can. It's up to you."

I didn't think I made a wise move there, but what choice did I have? I went to my cell to lay down 'cause I wasn't feeling too well. I lay down and fell right off to sleep. The next thing I knew, I was being awakened by Peggy, telling me it was supper time. I wasn't really hungry, but I knew I had to eat a little in case I was pregnant.

The guy who worked that night was real mean. He was a total jerk.

He had nothing nice to say to anyone. He thought that because he had authority, he could tell us what we could watch on TV and the whole nine yards. I couldn't take anymore of him, so I went to my cell and stayed there the rest of the night. I couldn't go to sleep at first. I just lay there looking at the ceiling, thinking about what was going to happen the next night. I couldn't wait to be free again. When I woke up the next morning, the sun was just coming up. It was going to be a nice day, the day I'd be free. I washed up in the sink in my cell, all the time humming to myself. After that, I sat on my bed and waited for the guard to come and unlock the door.

About an hour later, the guard unlocked the door and told me breakfast was ready. I felt like I hadn't eaten in days, and I was starving. I went out to the table in the TV room and got my tray and some eggs, bacon, and toast. I ate everything on the tray, then set it in the kitchen and went and sat down to watch TV. Kevin and Peggy were already sitting there watching something that looked boring, so I went and grabbed a book and sat down at the table.

Finally Pete showed up, and he was all smiles. I figured it was a good sign. After I hugged and kissed him, we sat down at the table. I couldn't wait to hear what he had to say. The way he was smiling, I just knew he had good news.

"Well, Sal, everything's planned for tonight at nine o'clock. Make sure you're ready to go when we come."

I stopped him there. Who was the "we"?

"Pete, wait a minute. You said 'we.' Who's the 'we' in this?"

He looked down to where our hands were on the table.

"Well, you know that one guy you really didn't care for at the Teen Challenge? Jason? Well, he's sorta helping us."

I couldn't believe this. First Peggy and now Jason. We were really asking for trouble now.

"Oh man, Pete. Now that's two extra people we'll have. Peggy wants to come, too. I told Kevin he could come, but I don't think he will."

"We'll manage; we always do. Now this is what's going to happen."

He explained to me no weapons would be involved. We would just make the guard go into one of the cells, and by the time anyone knew what was happening, we'd be long gone. It sounded good to me. I told him all I knew about the guy who'd be working that night, and he said everything sounded good and to hang in there and we would be together that night.

Once he was gone, I stayed to myself the rest of the day, wondering about how things were going to go that night. And when the guy came on his shift, I hoped nothing bad would happen to him. He was a black man in his early twenties. He brought in his jam box and played music and danced with us. He was real cool. He wasn't like the rest of the people who worked there; he let us have fun.

As the night wore on, I got more and more nervous. I didn't know if Pete would go through with this or if he would back out at the last minute. So I was pretty well on edge when it came time for him to be there. And when it happened, everything happened so fast. I heard a knock on the door, and I knew it was them.I got up from the table and went over to the couch and sat down. I watched as the guard went to answer it.

I heard Jason saying something about his car breaking down, and he was wondering if he could use the phone. The guard led them into the office, and I could see Jason but not Pete. I watched as Jason brought out a pair of nunchucks. I could hear him telling the guard to get down on the floor. I was scared they were going to hurt him, but then the guard took off out the door that had been left ajar, and Jason went running after him.

I got up off the couch and went to the door and looked out. I really couldn't see much until Pete came running up to where I was standing.

"Come on. Let's go," he screamed at me, and I turned to see Peggy standing at my side and pushing me ahead. We both took off running down the hill to where I saw Pete's car. Pete was there beside me, and when we heard Jason's voice, we both turned to look at him and my face went pure white.

"Get the damn gun and shoot the nigger."

I turned to Pete and grabbed his arm.

"No, Pete. Please. Let's just go and get the hell out of here. Come on, please."

"OK. Get in the car. Jason, come on. Kick in gear and let's go." Everyone jumped into the car, and we took off. I was in the back with Peggy, and when I thought we were going to go over the bridge and be in another state, Pete took a sharp right, and we hit a gravel road. He pulled into a field and hurried to shut the car and the lights off. A few seconds after that, we saw three cop cars fly over the bridge with their lights on. Everyone in the car let out a cry of relief. I reached over the seat and gave Pete a huge hug.

"We did it, baby. We did it." I was thrilled. I couldn't believe we had pulled it off.

"Yeah, we did. But if we don't get out of here, we're going to get caught."

I sat back down in the seat so he could pull out. Pete had brought us some different clothes but forgot to get shoes. I didn't really mind, though. I didn't care about anything except being with him.

After a while, Pete let Jason take the wheel and got into the back seat with me. We had a lot to talk about. For one, we had suspicions I was pregnant, but we didn't know for sure. We had to figure out what we were going to do if I was.

"Sally, do you realize the mistake we're making if you are pregnant? How are we going to take care of the baby and get it medical attention?"

He was bringing up things I had not thought about, but I did know one thing.

"Pete, there's one thing I won't do for no one, and that's give up my baby. If I am pregnant, there's no way I would give it up. In fact, I'm almost positive I'm going to have a kid."

He looked at me, at a loss for words. That's when I started really thinking about the baby. How was I going to take care of a baby being on the run? I lay my bead back against Pete and tried to forget about the problem for the time being.

CHAPTER 16

Once we got to Tennessee, things did not go well. We were only four miles from the Alabama state line when the car decided to quit. The guys got out and looked the car over. I didn't know what the hell they were talking about, so I stayed in the car.

"Sally, were going to have to go and see if we can find a hacksaw."

I just gave him a strange look and got out of the car.

"Hey, guys. There's some houses off over in that direction," Jason said and pointed off to our right.

"What do you think, Pete?" I asked him.

"I'm not sure."

"Well, if you ask me, I think we should just keep walking and get on the other side of the line," I said.

"Yeah, but then what are we going to do for a car? We can't walk all that distance."

"Why the hell not?" I said. "We can walk it. Hell, I've walked farther than that before. I think we should get rid of that gun, too."

While we were in Tennessee, the guys had tried selling the gun, but I told them it wasn't a good idea 'cause then the cops would know sooner where we were. I think Jason thought I was some sort of loony or something 'cause he gave me a strange look. I just gave up and let them do what they wanted.

"Yeah, I agree with you about the gun. We don't need that on us if we get caught. But right now, we had better catch up to Jason and Peggy."

He grabbed my hand and off we went. By the time we caught up to the others, they were already knocking on someone's door. No one answered, so he went to the next house. And when no one answered there either, he got mad.

"Damn it all. These people just don't want to open their damn stinking doors."

The next thing we knew, he was going back to the last house we had tried and going around to the side of the house.

"If they won't open their doors, then I'll just go in anyway."

We all looked at each other, not sure what to do. There was no way of stopping him, so we all just stood there. I was standing by the window that be had gone into, swinging it back and forth. All of a sudden, we heard a loud commotion in the house.

"Get your white trash ass out of my house."

Everything seemed to happen so fast, I couldn't believe it. Jason came flying out of the window, knocking me out of the way, and just as I was falling, I heard something whiz past my head. A shotgun had gone off, and that scared the hell out of me. The next thing I knew, Pete was picking me up, and off we were running. We ran through a little batch of woods and came out onto the freeway again. Jason was nowhere around.

I started screaming at Pete. "Damn you. I told you we should've kept walking. Now we don't know if Jason got hit or not. Dammit, Pete. Why did we have to bring these two with us? We would have been better off going alone."

I was so mad and scared; I knew for sure we were busted now. Pete wrapped me in his arms and told me everything would be OK. We started walking, with Peggy walking a few steps behind us. We walked maybe ten feet when Jason came walking out of the woods. That made my temper go even higher.

"You stupid fool. What was the matter with you? You could have gotten us all killed with your stupid shit." I didn't know what I was saying. I don't think I made any sense.

"Nah. We're all too ornery to die." Jason was being a smart ass. I hated that guy right then. I think that if I could have got away with murder, I would have killed him right then.

The two guys were talking about where they should go. I heard

Jason say he thought we all should stick to the freeway and try to hitch a ride.

"No, Pete. I think we should split up and hit the woods over there. That lady is bound to go to the cops, and it would be harder for them to catch us if we went in there and split up." They were crazy to want to stick to the road.

"No. I think Jason's right. We should stick to the road and hitch a ride. But first, Jason, you had better get rid of that gun."

To my surprise, Jason agreed and walked over to the woods and went in. The three of us had no idea where he had stuck it. He told us only that it was hidden real well and no one would be able to find it.

We had walked for only about maybe fifteen minutes when a white car pulled up behind us. We all knew it was the cops. At that point, it didn't bother me. I think I really didn't want to run anymore. I had my fill of running all the time. I watched as two police officers walked up to us.

"Come on, kids. It's time to go the station. You two go with him, and you two come with me," one of them told us. The first cop took the guys and talked to them and put them into the car then came back to us.

"I'm not saying nothing, so save your breath," I told the cops before they could say anything to us. One of the cops just shrugged his shoulders and put us in the car and told us we could talk down at the station. I was sitting between Pete and Peggy. Pete was holding my hand, and I was holding onto Peggy's.

We were at the police station for two days before we were sent back to Missouri. The guys went to the county jail, and Peggy and I went to the juvenile center we had broken out of.

It was hard at first admitting it was all for the best that we got caught, but I finally accepted I would not be on the streets for a long time to come. But what was hardest was seeing the guy who got beat up. At first, I wouldn't even look at him, but then he came to me in my cell. He sat down on my bed beside me and began to talk.

"I've noticed you won't talk to me or even look at me. You know I don't hate you for what happened. It's done and over with, so can we be friends again?" I couldn't believe this guy. Here he was sitting on my bed and asking me if we could be friends again. I felt ashamed of what had happened. But there was nothing that I could do to take back what had happened to him.

I was in total awe of him. Most people would have been madder than a hornet, but not this guy. He was ready to forgive what we had done to him.

"Look, man. It wasn't supposed to happen the way it did. You weren't supposed to get hurt." I didn't tell him anymore about what was supposed to happen, and he didn't ask.

"Well, from what I was told by Kevin, it was you who stopped them from shooting me." He smiled and nudged me in my ribs.

"You know, you're too damn forgiving for your own good," I told him, smiling up at him.

"Does this mean we're friends again?" He was smiling with this crooked grin. How could I tell him no.

I smiled back and said yes. But I knew we could never really be friends 'cause I didn't trust anyone who worked for the law. I wanted to tell him I was sorry, but it was too hard for me to get the words out. Those were two words I always had problems with.

I stayed in the juvenile center until I went to court to see if I was going to be tried as an adult or not. The day of the court hearing, I was still pissed off 'cause Peggy walked free of all charges. She was let out a few days earlier. I was hoping maybe I would have walked, too. But I didn't have that kind of luck. The woman who was the judge looked mean as hell when I sat down in the courtroom, and I watched her until it was my turn. I walked up to the table and sat down.

"By looking at your records, I see you have been in a lot of trouble since you were real young. Do you have anything to say on your behalf?"

I stood up so I could tell her what was on my mind, but she gave me no chance.

"Never mind. Sit back down. I don't have time to hear any of your nonsense. I hereby declare that you be tried as an adult." I couldn't believe her. but then again after all that I had done could I really blame her?

She slammed down the gavel like a hammer, and I was ushered out the door and put into a cop car. I was so stunned that it really didn't hit me until I was at the county jail being strip-searched.

After the fingerprinting and everything else was done, I was given a uniform to put on and shown to my cell. The guard opened a big steel door, and I walked in. To my left, there was a big bathroom that had a tub, a four-person shower, a sink, and a toilet. Then there was another door in front of me. Following the guard into the cells, I was surprised to see two cells were open. One of the cells had a TV, and that's where three girls were sitting when I came in.

"You must be the kid we were told was coming."

The woman who spoke to me was older. I figured she was in her fifties. I smiled and didn't say anything. I was too scared. Then the dark-haired woman who was younger came walking toward me. She wasn't much taller than I was, straight dark hair, kinda pretty in her own way.

"You'll be sharing a cell with me."

She told me to come with her, and she would help me make my bunk. Then she wanted to talk.

"What are you in here for?" She was being friendly enough, But I felt that she was being just plain out nosey. I had a lot to learn from the games that went on in the jail cell. I was to naive yet to know what those games were. I had been in jail before but when I was locked up anytime before I was always in a cell alone.

I really was in no mood to be talking, but I figured I should just get it out in the open and over with.

"My boyfriend broke me out of a juvenile center. We screwed the guy up pretty bad. Well, I should say the guy who was with us screwed him up while the rest of us watched."

We talked for a long time that night. She was in there for robbing a church with her old man and brother. I didn't care what she had done. That was her business not mine.

The next morning I was awakened by the matron. She was shaking me.

"Come on, Sally. You have to get up 'cause in one hour you're going to court." I hadn't slept very well the night before and it felt like I had just gotten to sleep when she came in.

I went to court the day before, and I couldn't figure out why I was going again.

"Why do I have to go again? I just went to court yesterday." I didn't understand why I was going to court for the second day in a row.

"Well, today, you go in front of the judge and see what you are being charged with."

I didn't think it would happen so soon. I got up and went in and took a hot bath. When the time came for me to go, I was all ready.

The guard came in and took me out into the hall. I was surprised to see Pete and Jason standing there. I was shackled to Pete and taken across the street to the courthouse. On the way, I talked to Pete, asking him how he was, not caring if the guard gave me dirty looks or not.

"Hey look, Sally, when we get into the courthouse, Jason and I have something to say to you. Not right now because I don't want the guard to hear." I had no idea what they wanted to say to me but by the look on Pete's face I could tell it was serious.

I said OK, and we walked the rest of the way in silence. After we got into the courtroom and were seated, Pete leaned over and whispered, "Jason and I want you to go state's evidence against us. This way you could go home and take care of the baby until I get out." I couldn't believe he would say that. I sat there looking at him like he had lost his mind. He wanted me to be a rat. No way in hell was I going to become a rat.

"No, Pete, I don't think so. If I went against you guys, then you could get more time than what you should get. No, I won't do it. I hope I won't go to prison, but if I do, then that's something I will have to deal with." He gave me a hard look. I just turned and looked the other way. I couldn't let him take all the blame. If it had not been for me he would not be locked up right now. I was to be blamed for had happened. If anyone should walk free it should be him. He only did what he did because he loved me. I never felt more guilt in my life as I did bringing him down with me. I kept wishing that we could go back in time so that

110

I could change things. I knew in my heart that this was going to be one guilt that I would carry in my heart for the rest of my life.

He got really angry with me, but I couldn't see him taking all the blame. I wouldn't listen to anymore he had to say. I sat there waiting for the judge to tell me what I was charged with.

Walking back to the jailhouse, I was still stunned by what the judge told me: Count I, Burglary, first degree; Count II, Armed Criminal Action; and Count Three, Assault, second degree. Bond was set at $15,000 for Count I, $25,000 for Count II, and $5,000 for Count III. I knew I would be sitting in jail until my court date 'cause there was no way Mom could come up with that kind of money. I went back to my cell feeling down in the dumps. I went straight to my cell and lay on my bunk. I felt like crying, but no tears would come. My cellmate came into the room to see if I was all right. And when I told her what had happened, she seemed truly caring about me.

"Hey look, Kim," I said. " When I go to prison, Where is my baby going to end up at?" I slapped my hand over my mouth. I couldn't believe I had let it slip out. She stared at me for a moment before she responded.

"You're saying you're pregnant?" She was in total shock, No one had a clue that I was pregnant.

I nodded and looked at her with pleading eyes.

"Promise me you won't tell anyone. It these people find out, they might make me get rid of it. And I figure that if I can hold out as long as I can before they find out, then it would be too late to get an abortion." I wanted to cry. I was so affraid that they would make me get an abortion and the thought of losing my baby was something that I could not handle.

"Calm down. If you are pregnant, it would do you no good to get upset and hurt the baby. Now, how far along do you think you are?"

"Well, I'm guessing, but I'm a month or two. I'm not really sure." I tried thinking back to when I thought that I conceived the baby and if I was right then that would make me two months pregnant. But I couldn't be a hundred percent sure.

"Well I will keep it a secret, But we have to tell the others. This way we all can keep an eye on you." I knew that she was trying to be helpful, I still did not want to tell anyone else.

"No! I don't need no one to keep an eye on me. I was big enough to get myself into this trouble, then I'll be big enough to take care of myself."

I hadn't meant to get so upset, but I didn't want anyone to feel pity for me 'cause I was pregnant.

"All right. I'll tell you what, I'll keep it a secret, but you have to eat right and get plenty of rest."

I laughed at her when she said that. "What better place to get plenty of rest?" I told her, laughing. We made a pact that moment to keep my pregnany a secret. At least for the time being.

The days seemed to pass slowly. There was nothing to do but watch TV and read books. Three months had passed since I was brought to the county jail, and I was getting bigger and bigger as the days went by. I didn't know how long I was going to be able to hide my pregnancy. The baby was already kicking and moving all around. I got such joy out of feeling it move.

But one day, I started throwing up and started throwing up blood. It wouldn't stop, so I called for Kim to come into the room.

"Kim, I keep puking up blood. Do you know what that's from?" I was really scared 'cause I kept thinking that there might be something wrong with the baby.

She didn't know and said, "I think we should tell someone so you could go get checked out. It could have something to do with the baby."

I agreed with her, so she went and got one of the cops. I was taken to the emergency room and examined. After the doctor was done, he looked at me and said flatly, "You are only a child having a child." He sounded so disgusted with me.

He looked over at the woman cop, and she asked him bluntly how far along I was.

"She's too far along to have an abortion, if that's what you're asking. I'll make an appointment with the local doctor, and they'll call you and let you know when it is. They also will be able to tell her when she is due." With that, he walked out of the room. It was like he didn't even want to look at me. Like I was some kind of disgrace or something.

At first, after the doctor told me I was pregnant and the woman cop sat there staring at me like I was some piece of dirt, I felt guilty for not saying anything. I couldn't explain it to her, let alone to myself.

The following day, I was taken to the doctor's office and found out I was due in April. The doctor told me I would be having a baby girl. I was happy, but I would have been more happy if he had told me I would have a boy. That's what I wanted. But I knew in my heart I would love the baby no matter what it was. I just wanted a healthy baby. The women in the jail were ever watchful over me. They loved to feel the baby moving. I hoped that now the judge would have some kind of mercy on me. That way, I could go home and raise my baby. In my heart I knew that I would not have that sort of luck. I had done to many terrible things and no matter how much this baby meant to me and how much I wanted to change, I knew that the judge would not believe me if I told him that I would change for my childs sake.

December 17, 1984, was the day I went to court to be sentenced. I was scared as all hell. It was dark out, and Pete and I were being sentenced together. He held my hand as I stood there hearing what the judge said.

"Ms. Sally Stilson, I hereby sentence you to five years in the women's state penitentiary. There you will do a maximum of three years before you are eligible for parole." I didn't hear what he said after that. Three years, Three years before I could go up for parole.

I saw red then. All I wanted to do was wrap my hands around that judge's neck and wring the breath out of him. I think if I could have, I would have killed him right then. He was going to seperate me from my baby. I knew it was going to happen. But maybe in the deepest part of my heart I was hoping that I would have gotten another chance to prove to them that I could change.

I hadn't heard what Pete got at first. After we were taken to a small room, and I heard Mom on the other end of the phone the guard handed me, I thought about Pete and what he got.

"Mom, I'm going to prison for a couple of years," I told her, and when she burst out crying, I started crying and couldn't talk anymore. Pete took the phone and talked to her. I heard him tell her he got seven years and had to do a maximum of three years. That made me cry even harder. This was the guy who would do anything, and this was where we stood, going to prison. How could I have done this to him, and to our child? Because of me this man that stood by me through all the heart ache and trouble now had lost his freedom.

Two days later, I was on my way to prison. Pete was on the same bus as I was, so we at least got one last chance to see each other before I was dropped off at the prison. I even got to give him one last kiss before I got off the bus. It was hard saying goodbye to him, but I had no choice. I took one last look at him just before I stepped out of the van. Some how I was feeling that this would be the last of us. Things were never going to be the same for me after this.

CHAPTER 17

As I got off the bus and walked through the gate, I noticed there was one big white building off to my right and a building off to my left with two other buildings behind that one. I was taken to the big white building. I was strip-searched and put into a small cell. I was in the orientation dorm, where all of the new girls went before they were sent up to one of the bigger dorms. I could hear commotion outside but had no clue what was going on. I laid on my bed trying not to think of what might be in store for me or my child.

That same day I was taken up to the infirmary to see the doctor. I was scared as hell, and when the steel gates slammed shut behind the guard, that scared me more. I was told to be seated on a bench and not to move, and that's when a blonde girl came up to me.

"Are you the fifteen-year-old kid that's pregnant? The one they brought in here today?"

I couldn't talk, so I just nodded my head. She went off walking and shouting at people about what the hell they were thinking when they brought such a young kid into prison. I just sat there watching her as she walked away. Then I watched as a black woman came walking through some gates, bandaged from her neck to her ear. She started talking to the blonde who had just asked me if I was the kid they brought in, and when I heard what she had to say, I about pissed all over myself.

"Yeah, that black bitch didn't cut too deep. I'll have a scar, but I'm ok." They both were laughing like it was some sort of joke or something. I could see no humor in getting cut on the throat.

Both the girls went walking off somewhere. I never wanted to go home as much as I did at that moment. I wished more than anything that I could have been home where I knew it was safe.

I never found out what the whole story was on that girl who had got cut. All I knew was that it was about one wouldn't stop harassing the other. The guards wouldn't stop it so the one lady took it in her own hands and tried to kill the other.

I was in the orientation dorm for only a couple of days. Then I was moved upstairs to Two Dorm. The dorm had no walls, so people could not have privacy. The beds were called cubicles. In the middle of the room, there were single beds, and along each of the walls, there were bunk beds. I was put in one of the middle ones. Because there were no bottom bunks along the walls.

As soon as the guard walked away, everyone came walking up to me, wanting to know what I had done and when I was going up for parole and where I was from. I answered their questions one at a time. They all seemed friendly enough, but I didn't trust any of them, at least not until I saw a familiar face. She was one of the women who I was with in the county jail. She was more like a grandmother than anything. She ended up taking me under her wing, so to speak. She watched over me like a mother hen. Making sure that everyone knew that they were not to mess with me.

A couple of days after I was there, I went down to supper with Patsy. We had gone through the line and had taken our trays back to one of the tables. We were sitting there talking when a white girl and a black girl came walking up to our table and stood right beside me. I looked up at the black girl and smiled when she smiled.

"Hey, pretty girl, are you going to let me be the daddy to your baby? I could make sure you're all set while you're in here." I think my mouth fell to the floor. I looked over at Patsy, and she was smiling. This was one thing that I had not expected.

I looked back to the girl and told her bluntly, "I really don't think so."

"You're just going to hurt my feelings, just like that, without thinking about it?" She looked like I had crushed her.

I didn't say anything to her, so she started walking away, and the white girl stopped and had to get her say in.

"You really know how to hurt someone don't you?"

I watched as she walked away and went over to where the black girl had sat down. They were staring at me, so I turned around and looked at Patsy. I felt uncomfortable with them staring at me.

"Will you quit laughing? It's not funny," I told her. I didn't see the humor in any of it.

She stopped long enough to tell me something. "I should have told you this would happen, but I didn't think anyone would approach you so soon." She starting laughing again, and I couldn't help but laugh with her.

I was getting used to prison life. I was going to school and cleaning the dorm. It wasn't too bad. New Year's had come and gone, and I thought things were going OK for me. The black girl who had approached me was always watching me all the time. I just ignored her.

But then in February of 1985, things started looking down for me. I was always going to the doctors. They kept telling me there was something wrong with the baby, and most likely she would turn out to be a handicapped child. I didn't care, though, as long as she would be alive. But the doctors had other things in mind. At one of my weekly visits, I was taken into one of the offices and sat down. Not long after that I watched as one of the doctors came into the room. He started telling all that was wrong with my baby.

"Your baby will most likely not be normal when she is born. She is not developing right. And I think you should consider adopting her out to a family that could give her the treatment she deserves."

I cut him off then. It was like a slap in the face. Adoption? That had never crossed my mind not even once.

"I am not putting my baby up for adoption. I have talked to my mom, and she said she would take her and take care of her. She will have all the love she could get, and it won't be from a bunch of strangers," I screamed at him.

"Sally, you don't understand. If this child is born not normal, then it is going to cost a lot to take care of her. You have to try and

117

understand what you are asking of your family."

When he said "if" the baby was born abnormal, that's when he made one of his mistakes. There was a chance my baby could be born normal, and even if she wasn't, I was still going to keep her. I was so mad at this doctor, my blood pressure went sky high.

"No, doctor. I don't think you understand. I'm not getting rid of my baby even if she is handicapped. She belongs to me and my boyfriend, and I'm not giving her away to no one except my mother."

I got up out of the chair and walked out into the hallway. The guard followed me. She took me back to the prison. I told Patsy what had happened. She was just as upset as I was.

"I can't believe they're doing this to you. But if I was you, I'd be calling your mother and telling her what the hell they're pulling. She could do a lot more than you can. Why don't you go and give her a quick call."

"Yeah. Maybe you're right." I was getting very confused. I couldn't believe the doctor wanted me to give up my baby. How could anyone ask a mother to give up their child. I realize that I am young, That doesn't stop me from loving my child.

I really didn't want to call her and get her all upset, but if I didn't, then God only knew what would happen. Patsy walked with up to the phone and stood there while I told Mom what was going on.

"Sally, whatever you do, do not sign no papers or nothing." She sounded like she was really worried. I could tell that she was upset.

As I was talking to Mom, one of the guards came up to the steel door and told me, "Sally, you have another doctor's appointment tomorrow morning. You'll be leaving here no later than seven in the morning."

Why was I going back to the doctor? I had gone there that morning, and it didn't make sense that I would be going back so soon. I said OK and told Mom what the guard had told me.

"What the hell is going on down there? Why would you be going back to the doctor so soon?" She didn't like the sound of what was going on anymore than I did.

"Mom, I'm really starting to get scared. I don't know what to do anymore. They keep telling me there's something wrong with the baby, and they want me to give her up, and I don't want to. Even if she's not normal, I don't care. I'll still love her and take care of her as soon as I am released. mom I dont want to give up my baby. And I know Pete wouldn't want me to either."

I was crying by that time, and Patsy was standing there patting my back. Mom told me to sit tight, and she was on her way down. She didn't know where she was going to get the money, But she would be there no matter what. I felt a little better knowing that she would be there.Yet I still felt like something fishy was really going on.

The next morning, I was up and ready to go to the doctor. I didn't know what they were doing that morning, but I didn't trust them. I was taken into the hospital and put in a hospital gown, then made to lay on a bed. They put an IV in my arm and had a monitor on my belly. I watched as the baby's heart began to beat. I lay there for almost a half-hour hour before the pain started. I couldn't catch my breath at first. The pain took me off guard.

I began to feel stomach pains and didn't know what was going on at first, but then it hit me that I was in labor. I began to scream at the nurse, and she told me everything was going to be all right, but I didn't believe her. I yanked the IV out of my arm and sat up. Oh my God what was happening? What were they doing?

Just then, Mom came walking into the room. I never felt so relieved to see her as I did at that moment. She came rushing over to me.

"Sally, what's wrong? Are you in pain?"

"Mom, I think I'm in labor? I'm having a lot of pain, and it hurts." I was crying as I doubled over in pain.

She stood up and started yelling at the nurse, telling her to get me something to stop the pain. At first the nurse just looked at her, but when the doctor came in and nodded his head to the nurse, she went and got me something. She gave me a shot in the backside, and not long after that pain began to go away. Mom told the doctor she wanted to speak to him in the hall, and she gave me my clothes to get dressed. The guard helped me get dressed, and when I was almost done, Mom came back into the room.

"Sally, I'll be over to the prison to see you in a little while, then we'll talk. Are you sure that you're OK?" She sounded so worried. I just wanted her to hold me and tell me that everything was going to be alright.

"Yeah. I'm OK. I'm not in pain no more," I told her with a smile. She told me not to worry 'cause she was going to take care of things. I knew she would try. The guard took me back to the prison, and I lay down after telling Patsy what had happened. She told me to lay down until Mom got there 'cause she thought I looked awfully pale. I was still laying on my bed when Mom came an hour later.

I went to the visiting room and saw she had another woman with her. Whom she introduced to me as a friend of hers.

"Sally, I want you to listen to me very carefully. I do not want you to talk to no one at the hospital, and you are not to sign no papers. Whatever you do, do not sign anything. Jackie and I came right here from the hospital, and we talked to the doctor, and he tried to convince me you should give your baby up for adoption 'cause it's not normal. But I don't trust that doctor, so you just watch what you do."

There was something Mom wasn't telling me. I could tell by the way she was looking at me. But I couldn't figure it out.

"Mom, what's really going on? I'm not giving up my baby. I won't. She's mine, and as soon as I'm out of here, I want to raise her."

"That's why you have to do what I tell you, or you are going to lose her." She went on telling me everything was going to be OK, and she stayed until visiting time was over. I told her I would be more careful, and if anything else happened I would call her. If I couldn't, then I would have someone else call her. She had to go back to Michigan that night, so I wouldn't see her until the baby was born. It was hard telling her good-bye. I felt better knowing when she was there. I knew that she would never let anyone hurt the child or me.

After that I was more careful when I went to the doctor. I told him only that I felt fine and the baby was moving a lot. And when he brought up about having my baby adopted, I just told him I hadn't changed my mind.

And then one day, I had an unexpected visitor. I was told to go to the lieutenant's office. I went down and walked into the office without knocking. There behind the desk was a woman who looked like some sort of matron. She had her hair pulled back in a tight knot at the back of her head and was dressed all in black. I sat down in the chair in front of the desk without saying anything. She set down the pen she was using and looked at me.

"I have some papers I need you to sign for your baby. It will help protect your baby as well as yourself." She sounded like a no nonsense sort of lady.

I sat there staring at her. I wasn't going to sign any papers, not for her or anyone else.

"Listen here, lady. I'm not signing no papers for you. All you're doing is wasting your time and your breath. You know where you can stick them papers." I wasn't being very nice to her, and I didn't care.

"Listen, Sally. This will be in the best interest of the baby and everyone concerned." She was doing everything in her power to be nice when all she really wanted to do was be mean and nasty.

That's when I knew she wanted me to sign my baby away.

"Listen here, you old bitch. I don't know where you think you have the right to tell me what to do with my baby. But to be honest with you, I really don't give a damn one way or the other. I'm not giving up my baby, and that's all there is to it."

I got up to leave.

"If you walk out that door, I will make sure you are put in the hole, pregnant and all."

My face went pure red.

"Go ahead. I don't care 'cause I'm still not signing no papers. And I will have my mom contacted, and she will be down here in no time flat." I walked to the door and opened it. But she still had to get the last word in.

"If you don't sign that baby away, you and the child will never amount to nothing is this life. You both will be nothing. Do you understand that?"

I slammed the door shut and went back to my dorm. I couldn't understand where these people thought they had the right to tell me what they thought was best for me. Sure, I committed a crime, but I was paying for what I had done, so why couldn't they just leave me alone. I lay on my bed and cried for a long time. Everyone thought I was sleeping, but all I wanted was to be left alone.

That night I went into labor. I couldn't get hold of Mom, and I wouldn't go until I could, but when Patsy came back to the dorm from the kitchen, she talked me into going to one of the guards and said Mom would be called by one of the girls.

By the time I got to the hospital, I thought I was going to die. I was in hard labor, and it seemed like all the doctors would do was sit around. They came into the room only to examine me and then walked out. I was in pain for about four hours when Mom showed up. After she walked in, the doctors and the nurses started getting something done. Mom somehow got them to stop the labor. I had no idea what she said to them but she got things done rather quickly.

I was out of it for about two days. I couldn't remember what had happened for those days. But I remember a different doctor coming in and giving me an ultrasound. he kept trying to keep me awake through the procedure. I kept falling back to sleep. I could dream there, I could dream of Pete and the baby. What things should have been like. Not what they really were. But this Dr. would not let me fall back into that dream state. He kept telling me that I had to get better for my babys sake.

"Do you want to know what you're going to have?" he asked me with a smile.

Mom spoke up. "We already know. The doctor told her she was going to have a little girl."

He shook his head and started laughing. "This is a funny-looking little girl. See here? This baby is a boy." He was pointing to the screen showing us that I was really having a boy.

I couldn't believe it. My dream was going to come true. I was going to have a little boy. As I fell back to sleep I could tell that I was smiling. The following day when I woke up I saw that mom was sitting in the corner sleeping. I could barely talk. My throat was so dry I had to whisper to her.

"Mom." I tried. But she didn't hear me. I tried a little louder.

"Mom." This time she heard me, She looked up at me and smiled as she walked over to the bed.

"You really gave us all quite a scare. How you feeling today?" I smiled up at her.

"I think Im ok. My mouth is really dry. Can I have something to drink?" She let me have a little sip, but told me not to gulp it.

"Is the baby alright?" I asked her.

She told me everything was going to be OK and not to worry about things.

"Sally, I have also got another doctor to take care of the rest of your pregnancy. And he says he's not going to let you out of the hospital until the baby is developed. He then will release you back to the prison. So I think you will be all right from here on out. Now I have to head back home for the other kids, but I will be back when the baby is born. All right?"

I didn't want her to leave but I knew I had no choice. All of this was breaking my heart. I knew she really didn't want to leave, She had no choice. She had four other children at home to take care of.

"I'll be OK, Mom. Really. I know you have to head back."

She kissed me on the cheek and gave me a hug and left. I cried 'cause i didn't want her to go. I felt so alone and scared. I kept thinking to myself, Thank God I have the little one with me for now. I knew I had to hand him over to Mom as soon as he was ready to leave the hospital, but for right then, at least I had him. Now that I knew that the baby was going to be OK I felt better then I had in a long time.

CHAPTER 18

I stayed in the hospital for nearly a month, from February 5 to 25, 1985. Upon my release, I was first taken back to the Women's Correctional Center to get some clothes. From there, I was taken to the maximum security prison for men. I had never been in there before, and I was surprised to see more gates than there were at the prison I was in. I was taken up to the infirmary where other women from the prison were. To my surprise, Patsy was one of the women who was there. She came up to me as I walked through the door.

"Hey, little one. How are you doing? You finally came back to us, huh," she said, smiling.

"Yeah, I had no choice. So how do you like staying here?" I asked her.

"Well, come on. I'll tell you all about it while we make your bed up." She grabbed an armful of sheets, blankets, and a pillow. I followed her into a little dingy room. It wasn't very clean, and it smelled. I wrinkled my nose at her and she laughed.

"I know it smells, Its better then being out there with the other women. At least you have a little privacy. More then I can say for the rest of us out there." She smiled.

"First thing you have to know, Sally, is we don't eat no food that comes from the kitchen. They jack off in the food."

She laughed when she looked up at me. I must have had a terrible look on my face.

"Oh, man. That's sick. How can they get away with that?" That was so sick. I couldn't believe the guards would let them get away with that.

"I don't know, but one of the guys told us when he brought the food to us. He was rather nice. He didn't have to tell us but like he said. No one should have that done to them. I guess you can say he felt sorry for us." She smiled.

"Then what do we eat around here?" I didn't know what I was going to eat because I knew I had to eat for the baby's sake. But there's no way I would eat what the guys brought.

"Well, we've all been living off the toast here. And then sometimes, the guards will bring in different stuff, but not very often. I guess the flood is slowly going down at the women's prison. And soon we'll be going back."

I was glad to hear the last part.

>From the time I was released until around March 1, we stayed at the men's prison. And when we were allowed to go back, we all were thrilled. I couldn't wait to get back and have a decent meal and a clean place to sleep. There were plenty of nights I sat there in bed watching cock roaches on the floor. I kept thinking that they were going to creep up on the bed. I couldn't handle the thought of bugs crawling on me.

Finally we were able to go back to the womens correctional center. All of us women were relieved to get out of the mens prison. That place was awful. You could hear the guys making sounds, making comments about what they would like to do to us. It was awful. So when the guards came and told us that we would be going back we all shouted for joy. I wasn't there as long as the other women but I was just as happy as they were.

We weren't back to the womens prison long when I first felt the labor pains. I was so scared that at first I didn't tell anyone that I was going into labor.

On March 3, I was in full labor again. I went into labor early that afternoon, but I didn't say anything until Patsy came back from the kitchen. In the meantime, I was trying all day to get hold of Mom but couldn't seem to reach her. Patsy was so upset with me she started yelling at me.

"Sally, what the hell are you doing? You should have told the guard, especially after all the trouble you have had with this baby."

"Patsy, don't even think about starting with me. I'm not going to no hospital until I get a hold of my mom. You know what they have been trying to do, so don't start with me." I snapped at her.

I didn't mean to snap at her but I was starting to get real scared 'cause I couldn't get hold of Mom, and I was starting to feel more and more pain. Sometimes I thought the pain was going to send me right through the roof. It hurt so badly, At times it took me a couple of minutes to catch my breath.

"All right, Sally. Calm down. What if I promise you one of us will get a hold of your mother for you and you go on to the hospital? How does that sound?"

I didn't like it, but the pains were getting closer and closer. I knew if I didn't get a move on, the baby would be born right there at the prison.

"OK, you win. But you have to promise me you won't quit trying to get a hold of her." She agreed and I was taken to the infirmary where I waited until the ambulance got there. At the hospital, I was put on a monitor, and my doctor came in to see how everything was going.

"Well, Sally, we're going to let you stay in labor. The baby is ready to be delivered, so we'll let you try and have it naturally." He was a good doctor. I liked him a lot. Ever since taking over as my doctor, he had never treated me any differently. He ignored the guard as she sat off in one corner. She stayed out of the nurse's and the doctors way.

I stayed in labor all night long. I could have only ice chips to suck on. When the guard thought I could handle something other than ice chips, she asked one of the nurses, "Couldn't she have some Seven-Up or something? Maybe a Popsicle?" I could tell the guard felt sorry for me. She would sit there rubbing my face with a wet cloth and talking to me like a mother would.

"It's ok Sally, Pretty soon this will all be over." She kept telling me that over and over again.

The nurse said I could have a Seven-Up, but I couldn't drink it too fast, just in little sips. The guard didn't even bother to handcuff me to the bed. She was suppose to. In my condition I wasn't going any where.

"I don't think you're going anywhere, and with you being in labor, it would only make you more uncomfortable."

I was relieved she didn't lock me down. I don't think I could have handled it. That night was one of the longest nights of my life. I was in so much pain that I couldn't sleep, and when I thought I could sleep, the pain would start back up.

At eight o'clock the next morning, the doctor broke my water bag and left me there in all the pain. I screamed at everyone who came near me. Sometime that afternoon, the woman who had came to see me at the prison came back again. She sat down beside me in the chair that was next to my bed.

"Sally, I think you should sign these papers now. It would be in the best interest of everyone." She was anxious, I could tell by the way she spoke and by the way she sat there fidgeting.

I looked at her and started screaming.

"Get the hell out of my face, you rotten old bitch. You couldn't do nothing before, and you ain't going to do nothing now."

I reached my arm out and swatted the papers she was holding out to me, and they all went flying in the air. The guard who was there stood up by my bed, and from the sound of her voice, I could tell she wasn't very happy with the woman.

"The girl says she won't sign no papers, so I suggest you remove yourself from this room."

The woman was so mad at me and the guard, her face was pure red. If I hadn't been in so much pain, I would have laughed at her.

"You will see that you are making one of the biggest mistakes of your life. You mark my words that you won't amount to nothing, and neither will that bastard of a child. Mark my words on that."

"Leave." The guard told her as she pointed to the door.

And with that, she walked out of my room. I didn't have time to dwell on what she had to say. The pain was more than I could handle at the moment. At four that afternoon, my doctor came walking into the room and started checking me over. The next thing I knew, he was yelling at everyone to get me into the delivery room 'cause the baby was stressing out or something like that. He leaned over my bed and talked to me soothingly.

127

"Sally, everything is going to be all right now. There's nothing to be scared about. It's the baby's heartbeat. It's not strong anymore, and I'm afraid that if we don't get you in there and take this child by an emergency cesarean, the baby will not make it."

I tried to understand what he was telling me but couldn't. I was rolled into another room. It felt cold. I fought hard so they could not strap me down at first, but they finally got me. Then I felt a warmth going through my arm, and I was out of it. I didn't know what time it was, but I remembered someone putting the baby in my arms. I kept saying I didn't want to 'cause I thought I was going to drop it. The next time I came to it was eight o'clock at night. The guard was sitting by the bed watching TV.

"Where's my baby?" I asked her. She jumped, startled, and came closer to the bed.

"You have a beautiful baby boy. Here, ring for the nurse, and she'll bring him down."

She handed me a buzzer, and not long after that, the nurse came walking in with my little boy. She placed him in my arms, and I stared at him. He was so little and precious. I began to cry. He was perfect all the way from his head to his little toes. I cuddled him up next to me, and that's where he stayed until the nurse came in and told me I had to get some rest. I let her take my little one, and I went back to sleep.

Mom showed up the following day with my younger brother and sister in tow. They couldn't get over how little he was.

"Mom, the doctor said that the baby can leave tomorrow." I told her ready to cry. I did not want to give him up.

"I know." Was all she could say at first.

She looked at me, and I could tell she was trying hard not to cry. It was hard for me not to cry. They stayed there most of that day, and when they headed back to the hotel, I took advantage of the rest of the time I was going to have with my little one. I named him after his father, and his two middle names came from the name of one of Pete's best friends.

That night, I fed him every feeding, and I changed him each time he needed it. I cried a lot that night. I didn't want to give up my baby.

I kept talking to him like he understood what I was saying. I wanted him to know so badly how much I loved him, How much I was going to miss him. I never imagined that I could love another human being as much as I loved this little boy laying in my arms.

At nine o'clock the next morning, Mom was there to get the baby. She watched as I signed the papers for the baby to be discharged and for her to take care of him until I was released, The hospital then gave her a bunch of diapers and formula and some other stuff for the baby. Then I had to get him dressed and ready to leave. But first the hospital took a picture of me and the baby. After I had the baby ready, I was put into a wheelchair and rolled downstairs. I kept looking at him with tears streaming down my face wishing more then ever that I could be going home with him.

By the time I handed my son over to Mom, everyone was crying, even the nurse who walked with us. I watched as Mom took my little boy, after giving me a hug and kiss, and walked out of the hospital. The nurse and the guard stayed there until we watched moms car dissappear. I felt so lost and alone.

I was lost without my little boy. I missed him after he had been gone only five minutes. I screamed at the nurses to get the baby stuff out of my room. The only thing I kept was one of the baby blankets I had wrapped him in when the nurses brought him in to me. For the next two days, I slept with that little blanket, but when I was released from the hospital, I couldn't take it with me. So I laid it on the bed when I left. God only knew how hard that was for me. I found comfort in that little blanket with his baby smell on it.

CHAPTER 19

After returning to the prison, I became very hard and bitter. I felt like I had no heart at all. But things got worse when Mom came about a month later. The visit went well, but I couldn't handle watching her leave with my son. I saw Mom that first year about three or four times. She couldn't make it down very often. She just didn't have the money to come. I tried to understand, But that was very difficult for me.

It didn't take long after being back at the prison for things to really change. Once my six week check up was over my life as I knew it would change forever.

I was beaten and sexually assaulted by other inmates, before I finally gave in and became one of them. I did what I had to do. I spent a lot of time in the hole for fighting or going off the deep end at one of the guards. I lived most of the time in the hole. The hole was nasty. We got to take a shower only three times a week, and for me that just wasn't enough. But I had to live with it. There was only one window, and that was way on the other end. The only thing you could do in there was read. And half the time, you didn't have enough light. So I lay on my bed and stared at the ceiling and talked to the other girls who were in there. You couldn't see anyone, but you could talk to them.

The things that I endured the first couple of times was unimaginable. I didn't think that after being in the prison for four months that I would go through the torment and sexual assault. I found out that the inmates were just waiting for me to have my baby. I was even told once that they had dibs on who would get to me first. I tried to fight them off, God knew I tried. I was to small. There was always more then one. I felt degraded and so ashamed. How could I ever look at Pete or any other man like I once did.

When mom would come and see me, she would sometimes bring Pete's mother and they both would tell me that I should marry Pete for the baby's sake. How could I tell them what had happened? How could I marry Pete? They had no idea what I was going through. I would never tell mom, I was affraid that she would try and carry the guilt. This all was my fault not hers. If I would have just stayed out of trouble then none of this would ever have happened.

When I finally agreed to marry Pete it didn't take long to get the papers around. Mom and Pete's mom went right away and got the papers ready. Now it was up to the prison to set up the day. Everyone seemed happy that I had decided to marry, All except me. The burden that I was carrying around made it that much more difficult.

In the meen time I kept getting sent back to the hole for fighting. When one of the guards approached me with the news of the wedding date.

"Well they tell me that you are to be married on October 21st." With that he walked away. In my mind I wanted to scream at him and tell him that I changed my mind. The thought of dissappointing mom again was something that I couldn't handle. Besides my son needed a father and a mother. Maybe once we were released from prison, Then just maybe we could work things out. I had to keep telling myself that in order to go through the wedding date. I couldn't see how things would work out, But then who knew.

The day I got married, I felt a dread deep inside. I never planned on getting married in a prison. I doubt if anyone ever does. I wore a pretty flowered shirt that I borrowed from one of the girls. Everyone kept saying how pretty I looked. When I looked in the mirror I couldn't see what they saw.

When the guard came and got me and told me it was time. I almost told her to forget about it. How was I going to look Pete in the face and not tell him what had happened? How was I suppose to go through with this? As I walked over to the visiting room I kept telling myself that I would have to tell him that there was no way that I was going to be able to marry him.

As I walked into the visiting room, Pete was sitting at one of the tables looking nervous. As he looked at me a big grin broke acrossed his face. I realized that there was no way that I could not marry him. He was so happy to see me I thought he was going to burst. "Hi." I said as I stood there. He slowly rose and before I knew it he gave me one of the biggest hugs that I have ever received. ""It is so good to see you babe." He stood a little back taking every inch of me in with his eyes. I just stood there smiling at him. "I thought for sure you would change your mind. I never get very many letters from you any more." He spoke softly. "I guess Im just busy is all." What was I suppose to say to him? "We get a couple of hours to visit after the marriage ceremony is over." He told me gently. After we took our vows, We sat there with him mostly talking about the future, Raising our son together and what a wonderful life we would have. I just agreed with him not feeling anything. I knew everything that he was talking about were all empty promises. I felt guilty, But I couldn't hurt him.

I stayed in lockdown until April of the following year, when I was moved upstairs. That's when I found out the women were being transferred to another prison. The prison I was in was coed, and they wanted to make it an all-men's facility. In May of 1986, I moved to the other prison. It was like a big college campus with seven buildings. One was the kitchen, and one was the rec area. The rest were dorms. I liked it so much better 'cause we had regular rooms. It was a lot better place to do time.

I became one of the other women. I had a girlfriend and did what they did. I did what I had to do. I wanted to survive, When you are in prison you do what ever it is that you have to do no matter what the cost. I didn't write to Pete much any more. After the wedding I just thought that it would be best just to let things go.

The rest of my time, I didn't get into much trouble. I got my G.E.D. and then went to work in the kitchen where I started out cooking. I then went down to the shipping and receiving area of the kitchen. I kept myself busy most of the time. It helped me to pass the time.

Mom visited when she could. It hurt a lot that my son didn't know me and wouldn't come too close to me, but I didn't sit and dwell on it. My time was getting shorter and shorter, and I figured I would have enough time to make up for all of the lost time when I got home.

When I wasn't working, I spent most of my time working out in the weightlifting room. Sometimes, I watched movies or went swimming, when the pool was open. I tried to keep myself busy. I hated to have to sit and think about everything that had gone on up to that point.

Most of all, I hated to think about Pete. I no longer had his pictures up. I had taken them down before I went to the new prison, and I never put them back up. I had married Pete back in 1985, and I regretted it. He was brought to the prison I was in, and we got married there. I married him 'cause I thought I was doing the right thing for my little boy. But I knew I only did it for my mom. She wanted me to marry Pete for the baby, and she talked me into it. But I no longer felt the same for him. Mom said she thought it was because I was locked away, and maybe I would feel different when I got out. But the closer I got to getting out, the more I knew I didn't feel the same. And that made me feel guilty 'cause I thought I owed it to him after all that he had done for me. So, instead of thinking about it, I kept myself busy.

In September 1987, I went up for parole. Mom came down to be there for me, and so did my mother-in-law and, of course, my son. Mom went in with me, and she did most of the talking.

"I believe my daughter has learned her lesson, and I don't think she will give the law any more trouble," she told the parole board. "I believe she will try harder to do better. I know she is not perfect, but I believe with all my heart that after all she has gone through, she will no longer get into trouble. Sally and I have become closer since this whole ordeal. She knows she can turn to me and talk to me now. I love my daughter, and I would love to see her come home and raise her son and build a life with him."

One of the board members looked right at me and asked, "Do you believe you have learned your lesson? What have you learned about being incarcerated?"

I didn't hesitate in my answer.

"Sir, I have learned it isn't worth committing a crime and losing not only your freedom, but in my case I lost my son for the first two and a half years of his life. I have learned that it's not worth running from your problems and that there's someone out there willing to listen."

I looked him straight in the eyes while I was talking. When it was all over, Mom and I walked back over to the prison and visited the rest of the morning. She was going to Pete's hearing that afternoon, so she had to leave early enough to get there on time. She told me to hang in there and she would see me the following day.

We had a good visit the next day when she came. I enjoyed seeing her. Before she left, she hugged me and kissed my cheek and simply told me, "You'll be home soon, so just hang in there." She smiled at me, and I knew somehow she was right. I would be going home soon. I just knew I would be. She had told me things went real well at Pete's hearing, but that did not change my mind about him. I felt happy for him, but that was all. One week later, I got my parole papers back from the hearing. I was called down to the office of the woman who took care of that and was shown the papers.

CHAPTER 20

"You're to be paroled any day, Sally. All we have to do is wait for everything to be done up in Michigan. And as soon as we hear, then you will be released."

I was thrilled. After three years and four months of being locked up, I was finally going home. I ran to the kitchen and told everyone. They all seemed happy for me but the one cook.

"Yeah, you'll be back. All you cocky ones are." She scoffed.

She was a bitch anyway, so I really didn't care what she thought, or anyone, for that matter. I was going home, and that was all I cared about.

I knew I was going to miss my friends, but I didn't realize just how much.

It was October, 5, 1987; the day I had longed for had finally arrived. I stood by my bed for the last roll call before I was to walk out of the gates.

"Good luck out there in the free world, Sal. Don't forget about all of us in here," my roommate told me as she walked out of the room to go to work. I thought I was going to cry.

I got my things together and before I walked out, took one last look around the one place I had called home.

Most of my friends were waiting at Donnelley Dorm. I hugged each one of them, crying the whole time. I was slowly walked out to the front gate, where my mother and sister and my son were waiting for me.

I turned around and looked at the prison one last time before I was finally convinced I was leaving and went to my mother's car.

After being released from prison, I kept in touch with a few of the women. One for sure, 'cause she was my girlfriend. But we eventually grew apart.

EPILOGUE

It has been several years since I have been released from prison. Since then I have never gotten into trouble with the law again. I got divorced after I was released. From my understanding Pete is doing well has other children and is remarried. As for myself my mother and I are closer then we ever have been. It took us a while to get there, But because of her I got the chance to finish raising my son.

I now am remarried and have four children. My life has turned completely around. I feel that if I hadn't gone to prison I wouldn't be the person that I am today. Now that I am a mother, I understand more of the things that my mother tried doing for me were the right things.

Printed in the United States
32180LVS00002B/73-114